THE CALL OF

INTERCESSION

From His Heart to Yours

Deborah

571
BEGAN

THE CALL OF

INTERCESSION

DEBORAH G. HUNTER

Hunter Heart Publishing
DuPont, Washington 98327

Hunter Heart Publishing, LLC
P.O. Box 354
DuPont, Washington 98327
www.hunterheartpublishing.com

Cover designer: Exousia Marketing Group, LLC
www.exousiamg.com

The word satan is not capitalized in this work. This does defy the basic rules of grammatical expression, but we have chosen not to highlight this name due to the nature of his character. There are instances of capitalization throughout the text that are used to emphasize the nature of certain statements.

~DEDICATION~

I dedicate this to all of the intercessors out there who take up their cross daily to stand in the gap for the things that are on the heart of God in this hour. Your countless acts of obedience and labors of love may never be acknowledged in this earth, but God has a great reward on the other side; set aside just for you.
~An Intercessor

❧ACKNOWLEDGMENTS❧

I want to acknowledge an awesome woman of God who mentored me through some of the greatest tests in my walk with the Lord, as He was calling me to my assignment to intercede for the nations. As an intercessor herself, she displayed such wisdom and grace as she taught, corrected, and mentored me through her own walk.

She never had to tell me much, she just spoke through her commitment and faithfulness in her own assignment, as well as giving me *the Word only*, and this was the only teaching that I needed.

She does not fully know the impact that she has had on my assignment as an intercessor, but she was a divine covering that the Lord ordained over my life. I will be forever grateful for the love, friendship, and covering that you have been in my life.

Hilary Amara, may the Lord give you the reward that only He can give.

The greatest mentors are seen and not heard.
-Deborah G. Hunter

✑FOREWORD✑

In this hour of Apostolic Reformation, we discover that God is reconciling the nations of the world unto Himself through The Church, and intercession is key to this redemptive assignment. Intercession is the critical redemptive function that is often devalued, misunderstood, and marginalized in our Western Christian culture. Therefore, many Christians never make the connection between strategic corporate intercessions and manifested earthly outcomes. We have clearly embraced the role of preaching, teaching, and practical outreach, but have somehow failed to grasp the preeminence of intercession in the scope of redemptive work. Debbie Hunter has demonstrated through The Call of Intercession that she has made this connection, and clearly possesses profound insight into the intercessory function and calling of The Church of our Lord Jesus Christ.

Debbie Hunter is an extraordinary Christian woman who has made her life's assignment the pursuit of intercessory dimensions. As readers engage The Call of Intercession, they are taken on a journey into the private and holy chambers of the heart of this author who, by the aid of the Holy Spirit, is able to express the mind of God as it relates to this unique and significant assignment of prayer and intimacy with God. Debbie has penned a great and substantive body of work as an inspirational and instructional tool for those fellow believers who are called to explore the depths of prophetic intercession, holiness, and devotion to God.

This work gives us a glimpse of the awesome nature of a life surrendered to the burden of loving and caring for humanity to the extent that intercessions are offered faithfully on their behalf. Skillfully, the author lays out the Biblical mandate for keeping the assignment of the Lord's Watch through intercession, and provokes her reading audience to join in this watch. The author clearly proposes that in this hour, intercessors must take up the global mantle to pray for the nations of the earth in keeping with God's desire and love for humanity.

Dr. Keira Taylor-Banks
Executive Pastor, Living Waters Christian Fellowship
Newport News, Virginia, www.keirabanks.org
Author of *The Matriarchal Dimension:*
Positioning Spiritual Mothers and Prophetic Women
For Destiny

❧Introduction❧

"So I sought for a man among them who would make a wall, and stand in the gap before Me on behalf of the land, that I should not destroy it; but I found no one."

Ezekiel 22:30

Throughout history, God has sought out for a man in the earth who would cry out for His people. If we take a glance back in time, during the period after the fall of man, we immediately see that God had a man in *'position'* to intercede.

Now before this, God had become enraged with man, because of the great wickedness that was spreading throughout the earth. The sons of God were taking the daughters of men to be their wives, and they did evil in the sight of the Lord continually.

"And the Lord was sorry that He had made man on the earth, and He was grieved in His heart." Genesis 6:6

The Lord had become so sorry that He had created man that He decided to destroy him from the face of the earth, along with every beast, creeping thing, and bird of the air. The Word says that there was one man who found grace and favor in the Lord's eyes and his name was Noah. Can you imagine that in the entire world, there was only one man who pleased God to the extent that He would preserve the earth because of his righteousness?

Noah had three sons; Shem, Ham, and Japheth and these, with their wives, replenished the earth after the Flood. Different nations descended from each of these brothers, but the nation that came from Noah's son Shem, produced a man by the name of Abram. Abram was chosen by God as the man in whom all the families of the earth were to be blessed. He was called "out" of his own country to a place that God would soon show to him. What great faith and trust in the Lord; where a man would uproot his entire family, possessions, and livestock and move out on just a Word from the Lord! If we go back just a little, we see a similar pattern acted out by Abram's grandfather, Noah.

The Lord eventually changed Abram's name to Abraham, being a father of many nations. *"No longer shall your name be called Abram, but your name shall be Abraham; for I have made you a father of many nations." Genesis 17:5*

God establishes His covenant with Abraham and declares to him all that He desired of him and his descendants after him. The word covenant is defined as an agreement; usually formal, between two or more persons to do or not to do something specified. God uses this term covenant very differently. The word covenant is the Hebrew word *beriyth*, which is defined as cutting; as in cutting or passing between pieces of flesh. This is a powerful demonstration of God's agreement with us, in comparison with man's views on covenant partnership. Agreements in the natural, as we have been taught, are made to be broken, but God; in His infinite wisdom, creates a covenant that once agreed upon, creates a *cutting away* of natural tendencies to give up or throw in the towel.

When you enter into covenant with the Lord, He sees you as His partner. He has promised things over your life; therefore, causing you to have access to Him continually. Abraham gained this access to the Lord through his obedience in fulfilling his part of the covenant. Abraham, because he covenanted with the Lord, subsequently agreed to sacrifice his only son Isaac on the altar. This was a symbol of *"cutting away of the flesh"*, or of crucifying the flesh; not being moved by his feelings or emotions, but trusting fully on the Word that God had spoken to him, as well as the covenant that the two had made.

*"**Then the Lord** appeared to him by the terebinth trees of Mamre, as he was sitting in the tent door in the heat of the day. Genesis 18:1 (emphasis mine)*

We see in this scripture that it says, *"Then the Lord..."* Only when we are obedient to carry out our end of the bargain or our part of the covenant, will God move on our behalf. More often than not, we expect God to answer our prayers or bless us when we have not even fulfilled our promises to Him or obeyed what He has told us to do first.

Abraham was very precious to God and God trusted him and because of this "partnership", He allowed Abraham to reason with Him for the people of Sodom. The Lord saw the great wickedness that was in the city and had sent the angels to destroy it. The men went on their way towards Sodom, but Abraham continued to stand before the Lord interceding for the city. He asked the Lord if He would destroy the righteous with the wicked.

"Suppose there were fifty righteous within the city; would you also destroy the place and not spare it for the fifty righteous that were in it?" Genesis 18:24

Abraham went on to say that the Judge of the earth should not do to the righteous what He would do to the wicked, and God *agreed* with Abraham. He said that if there were found fifty righteous men in the city of Sodom, that He would spare the place for their sakes. They continued to reason together, until they reached the conclusion that if there were only ten righteous people in Sodom, God would not by any means destroy the city. Abraham could be characterized in this instance as a "pesky" child who does not know when to stop being worrisome. But God saw this not as being worrisome, but as being passionate about a people and passionate about justice taking place. Sodom and Gomorrah were destroyed, but not until Abraham's cousin Lot and his family were escorted out of the city by the angels. There were literally less than five righteous people found in this city, but only three made it out alive.

*"And it came to pass when God destroyed the cities of the plain, that God **remembered** Abraham, and sent Lot out of the midst of the overthrow, when He overthrew the cities in which Lot dwelt."* Genesis 19:29(emphasis mine)

God remembered when Abraham had interceded, so He spared his family from ultimate destruction. Have you been so passionate about an issue that you became that "pesky" little child crying out to God to fix it? We must understand that in this hour, intercession is paramount to God's plans being established in the earth. We have to open our mouths and begin to declare what the Lord is saying to us in our quiet times of interceding for the nations. The Word of God tells us that we are to watch for the signs of the coming of the Lord. If we just open up our eyes and look at the world today, we will see what the Bible is speaking of. Time is of the essence and we have to stand our watch and not be deceived by the enemy. He knows that his time is short and he is out to cause as much havoc as he possibly can before that great and marvelous day when the Lord appears for His sons. Let us be ready at all times to hear from the Lord and to intercede for what is taking place in the earth at this time. It is right before us; all that the Bible speaks of is at hand.

"Nation will go to war against nation, and kingdom against kingdom. There will be earthquakes in many parts of the world, as well as famines. But this is only the first of the birth pains, with more to come." Mark 13:8 (NLT)

Birth pains in this text are representative of sorrows and travail taking place in the earth realm in this last hour. The Holy Spirit revealed to me that these birth pains are the various *"natural disasters"*, if you will, that are now affecting our entire world. Whether there be earthquakes, tornadoes, hurricanes, cyclones, tsunamis, or flooding; disease, famine, murders, or war; we see them as just mere acts of nature; whether physical or innate, but in the spiritual realm, there is warfare taking place in the heavenlies. This warfare is not taking place directly in heaven, but in the heavenlies, or the atmosphere directly above the earth. This is the area where satan and his angels reside. As the warfare intensifies in the heavenlies, so will we see the *"birth pains"* in the earth intensify. We must be willing to stand in the gap and intercede that God's will be done in the earth.

God's people will rise in this hour and begin to know who they are, so as to take their proper positions in the realm of the Spirit, and move mightily on behalf of God to reach the many lost souls of the world for the Kingdom of God. This is not a time to be timid, nor a time to just have church as usual. The body of Christ has been misunderstood for long enough. It is time to rise in the power of God's Spirit that dwells on the inside of us and allow Him to use us for His glory in the earth. Thousands upon thousands and millions upon millions of people are dying daily in their sin. We, as the people of God, have to catch the heart of God for His people and begin to love them as He loves them. It is time out for judgment. This is not our job. Our job is to love and pray for those who do not know the Lord and to teach them in the way that they should go, so that we can produce a generation of believers who will carry the Gospel of Jesus Christ to their generation and the generations to come.

Let us stand our ground and set up our posts. We are in a spiritual battle for the Kingdom of God. We have been taught for so long that once we become saved that life is a bouquet of roses and that we are to wait on our glorious trip to heaven. No! We have an assignment to fulfill in the earth. Our man of God tells us all of the time, *"If it were God's plan to just save us, then once we became saved, we would have been taken immediately to heaven."* As we are obedient to the assignment, God will move greatly in the earth and restore His Kingdom and regain the souls that are His. As an intercessor, you can move in this great assignment and still live a fulfilling life in this world. God will open up the windows of heaven over your life and allow you to obtain favor from the most unsuspecting people. You must understand that when God sends the vision; He must supply the provision for it. God has already done His part; now it is time for you to carry out your end of the bargain.

I realized my call to intercession through my woman of God. If you are not sure that you are called in this area, look at the pattern of your life and your prayer life. If you see that God is calling you to cover people and situations that you are not close to, as well as being prompted by the Holy Spirit to pray at a moment's notice, then you may very well be called into the ministry of intercession. We are all called to intercede, but we are seeing a remnant of individuals in the earth who are stepping out and moving in the full power of God in this area. I read some wonderful books about dreams and dream interpretation by Dr. Joe Ibojie, one entitled *Dreams and Visions*[1] and it opened my eyes to many things that I have experienced over my lifetime. I have always had dreams, even from childhood, and they have stayed with me throughout my life. As I studied these books, I found that God was calling me even as a child. I would have many dreams that I did not understand, but after studying both of these works; I finally knew what they meant. I had a dream in 2003 before I came to Germany to meet my husband. I was walking with my son attached to my chest in a baby harness, and as I looked up, I saw warplanes hovering overhead and they were shooting at me. I was shot, and I hit the ground. As I read these books, they revealed that warplanes were significant of a calling to the intercessory ministry, and the Lord shared with me that it would take a "dying" to self to begin operating in this anointing. It was soon after this that I was led to the ministry in Germany where it was confirmed to me that God was calling me to intercede for the nations.

If you have experienced such, or you feel that you are called in the area of intercession, avail yourself to the reading of this book, and allow the Spirit of God to minister to you through these pages. If you know of someone who is moving in the ministry of intercession, and are not sure that they are called, please extend this book to them, so that they can find themselves in the pages of this book. We all need to know from others who are walking in the same anointing, their experiences, so that we can sharpen one another's ministry.

Something great in the spiritual realm is released through the travail of an intercessor. Though He could not find an intercessor in the days of old to stand in the gap for His people, there is now emerging an army of intercessors standing in the gateways, taking their watch on the walls, and holding themselves up in the towers, ready to move out and change the atmosphere of the earth. Once we begin to understand that we are "On Assignment", our entire perception of this life will change, and we will begin to accept the call to intercede for this earth.

We have to see that it takes only one person; one submitted, committed, and obedient person to change God's mind on behalf of this earth and His people. If you know that the Lord is calling you to another level of intercession, prepare your heart to receive greater levels of insight, illumination, and revelation, as it pertains to the ministry of intercession. Will you answer the call?

❧ TABLE OF CONTENTS ❧

A LOVE FOR THE LOST

"What man of you, having a hundred sheep, if he loses one of them, does not leave the ninety-nine in the wilderness, and go after the one which is lost until he finds it?"

Luke 15:4

When I first gave my life to the Lord, I knew what it meant to be loved. I developed a great burden in my heart for the unsaved. I always found myself reaching out to those who seemed to be struggling in their everyday lives with the simplest things, such as love, joy, and having peace. This was not only among the unsaved, but among Christians who did not really know or experience the love of Christ for themselves. I always found myself clinging to an individual who just could not seem to grasp the fact that Jesus loved them. I would continuously encourage them that God was for them and that He sent His only Son to die for them. The passion in my heart for these people grew stronger by the day.

We saw from Abraham that he had such compassion for the people of Sodom that he reasoned with the God of heaven on their behalves. He mentioned several times in Genesis 18 that he was not worthy to even come before God.

The Call of Intercession

"And Abraham answered and said, 'Indeed now, I who am but dust and ashes have taken it upon myself to speak to the Lord."
Genesis 18:27

The Lord never judged Abraham or condemned him for speaking so honestly with Him, because He had made a covenant with Abraham; they were in relationship. This is how God desires for us all to be with Him. He desires to fellowship intimately with each of us in whom He created, so as to fulfill His plan in the earth.

Abraham had a burden in his heart for the righteous people of Sodom and risked his own life, not knowing how God would respond, to intercede for them. God recognized the level of his passion for these people and his willingness to sacrifice his own life to intercede for them, in hope that God would intervene. This is powerful! Abraham did not even know for sure that God would listen to him, but he stepped out in great faith for the people of Sodom and consequently, saved the righteous of that city. How much more do you think God desires for us to intercede for the lost of this world? He sent His only Son to die on a cross, so that every one of us would have a way to Him; man, woman, and child.

There should be such urgency on the inside of us to witness Jesus to the lost. Many times when we come across those who do not know the Lord we, as believers, find ourselves debating with them or trying to force them to go to our church. This is not how God desires for us to witness. In fact, this is not a true witness at all. When Jesus walked upon the earth, people drew near to Him, because of the genuine love that permeated His entire being. He did not just love; He was love! Glory to God! He loved people to Himself. Instead of judging them for what it was that they were doing wrong, or debating with them about who was right, He loved them to the point where they felt they had no other choice but to follow Him. This is powerful! Love is the single most important characteristic that a believer should possess. We carry the very same power on the inside of us that Jesus had in Him. More than that, the Word says that we have the power here on earth to go beyond the exploits of Jesus.

"Most assuredly, I say to you, he who believes in Me, the works that I do he will do also, and greater works than these he will do, because I go to My Father." John 14:12

People were laying down their old lifestyles and careers in an instant and following this man whom they did not even know. He had something on Him that they could not deny. The power of the anointing on His life caused people to give up families, businesses, and status to follow, as well as imitate this man called Jesus. This is the kind of love that God desires for us to possess; a drawing love. Our main purpose for being in this earth is to draw others to Christ. We allow ourselves to get so caught up in the "lusts of this world" that we lose sight of the mission; "To love others to Christ."

My sister Sandi was this type of person for me. You could see the love of Christ seeping out of her soul. Whenever I saw her, she was always smiling and extending her love to others. No matter what foolishness I may have been in at the time, she loved me and never judged me. It was not too long before I was drawn back to Christ through her love for Him, as well as for me. It is exactly that kind of love that has kept me pressing on in the Lord to this very day. She served as an intricate piece to the puzzle of my life, and without that very important piece; my life could have ended up very differently. We have been given assignments by the Lord in this earth. He has ordained a specific group of people in whom you will witness Him to. Before the foundations of the world, He knew whom you would come in contact with. He knew ahead of time the lives that you would touch through His love.

As believers, we have to learn how to move out of the "pew" and into position where God is able to use us for His glory. We have become so complacent in our walk with God that we have become satisfied with fellowship within the four walls of the "church" and missed the entire point of the Great Commission that God sent us out to fulfill. We missed the revelation that we are the church, not an actual building.

The Call of Intercession

"Go ye therefore, and teach all nations, baptizing them in the name of the Father, and of the Son, and of the Holy Ghost. Teaching them to observe all things whatsoever I have commanded you: and, lo, I am with you always, even unto the end of the world. Amen."
Matthew 28:19-20, KJV

We have to have the same passion on the inside of us for the lost of this world, just as Jesus did. We should love others so much that it hurts us to see them living in sin. We should display such compassion and acceptance of them, where they are drawn "out" of that sin by the love of God that dwells on the inside of us. We possess power and authority far beyond what we accept in this natural world. The problem with us is that we believe that it is in our own power that we will accomplish such things, instead of the powerful and living Spirit of God that dwells in us. We must accept that He has already done it and received the victory in the spiritual realm. We have to trust it, know it, see it, and then do it in the natural.

There are souls that are waiting for you to come and rescue them from the torment that they are living in, or in reality; dying in. If you are not walking in the will of God for your life and fulfilling the very purpose for which you were created, the souls that God has assigned you to will perish. I know that this may sound outrageous to some, but God created a people who will be directly affected by your calling or ministry.

The very things that you came out of; someone else has either gone through it also, is going through it, or about to go through it. God delivered you out of it, so that you could bring others out. The same hell that you experienced; someone else can and will go through if you stand back and do nothing. Do you want others to experience the pain and hurt that you had to endure? Do you want others to suffer needlessly when God has given you the answer for them? We must stop being a selfish people; only worrying about God blessing and increasing us and our family, and begin to display selflessness and seek to serve those around us as Jesus did.

One important aspect of being able to love the lost of this world is by having an intimate prayer life. If you do not spend quality time in the presence of the Lord, you cannot come "out" of yourself long enough to see into someone else's pain. You must first know that you know that Jesus loves you and has sacrificed His life for you first before you can go out and effectively win the lost to Christ. It is in your light that they find their way to God.

"Let your light so shine before men, that they may see your good works and glorify your Father in heaven." Matthew 5:16

I realized very early on in my walk with God that it was not about me, but about others. It seemed as if every time I was faced with a problem, God would bring someone else into my life who was dealing with something very similar. Here I was ministering to their need, while the Holy Spirit was ministering to mine. This has taken place more times than I can count and it revealed to me a great deal about the ministry that God has placed on the inside of me.

To truly have a heart for souls, you must be able to look beyond the person himself and see him as God sees him. This again, can only be developed through an active prayer life. As you lay before the Lord in prayer, God will speak to you through His Holy Spirit concerning someone. He opens up to you things that you would normally not "see" in a person. More importantly than this, you must display a consistent attitude of meditation upon the Word of God. You do not even begin to know who you are until you read it in the Word of God, so how can you effectively love another soul, until you are able to first love yourself and see yourself as God sees you?

It is also through the Word of God that we find our purpose in life, so if we know that we are on "assignment" and not on vacation, then we can effectively be used by God to reach the lost of this world. To love in such a way requires a great deal of sacrifice and selflessness. You should always be ready for God to send you directly into the pathway of those whom He desires for you to witness to. You should be willing to drop whatever it is that you are doing at a moment's notice, to minister to the need of that individual.

If you are single, then this allows you more of a freedom to be used by God, so take this as a privilege. As a man or woman of God who is not married, you do not have to restrict yourself to other commitments, but only to the service of the Lord. Nevertheless, if you are married, this does not disqualify you for ministering effectively to the lost. I am a perfect example and because I know me, I am able to share my experiences. The Lord has placed a great burden in my heart for His people. I used to watch television specials where missionaries would travel all over the world helping the poor and needy. I felt helpless, because I was not able to travel as they were and thought that I could never do anything to help. God began to speak to me through His Holy Spirit that I had many things at my disposal, including that of prayer.

My prayer life began to grow almost instantly. I stayed in the Father's face, seeking Him as to how He desired for me to help His people. In this time, I began to see His children as He saw them and He would show me how much He loved them, as well as me. Because I submitted myself to the Lord in prayer and spent quality time in His presence, people drew to me; not necessarily to me, but to the God that was so evident on the inside of me. This is a saying that a precious man of God says, "When the squeeze is on, whatever is on the inside will come out." We should purpose to stay in the presence of the Lord in prayer, so that when the trials and tribulations of this world come, only He will come out of us.

This is one of the greatest witnesses to a lost and suffering world; your testimony. When you are able to share with others what God has brought you out of, it gives them hope that their situations are not hopeless. God allows us all to go through different trials not only to strengthen us, but to bring someone else out as well. Never look at your situations and say, "Lord, why are you letting this happen to me?" Instead, begin asking Him, "Ok Lord, who is this for?" "What is my assignment?"

When you are able to view your life as an "assignment", God will use you mightily to reach His people. You become mission focused and your life begins to take on purpose. Now to effectively carry out the mission, you must first know what the mission is. Again, look back on Matthew 28:19-20, which gives us the Great Commission. We must know the Word of God in order to show others that they are lost. Now I am not saying to tell people that they are lost. We must also seek the wisdom of God in all things. What I am saying is that you, in and of yourself, cannot pull others out of the fire, but the Word of God is able to shine light on those dark places and penetrate where mere words or opinions cannot.

The one thing that changes people's lives and transforms their mindsets is the Word of God and usually, the only way that they will open up to accept it, is through the love of God that you express and extend towards them.

"Bless the Lord, you His angels, who excel in strength, who do His word, heeding the voice of His word." Psalm 103:20

When you love someone who is hurting or going through hard times by speaking a word into their lives, angels are automatically released into their situations. There is power in your words and the angels heed the voice of His word and perform that which was spoken. Now this is not a word that comes directly from God. God can only move in the earth realm through a submitted vessel. He needs a man in the earth who will move on His behalf in the lives of His people. This is why it is so very important that we speak the Word only and not give our mere opinions, unless those opinions line up with the Word of God. This can come down to life or death for someone. The word of God in Proverbs 18:21 says, "Death and life are in the power of the tongue, and those who love it will eat its fruit." Right here is the place where you will find out whether God has sent you, or you yourself have taken it upon yourself to do God's job for Him.

Yes, God speaks to us to go forth and spread the Gospel, but there is a process that we all have to go through in order to effectively reach His sheep. We have to allow Christ to develop us through the Word of God first before we try to go out and teach something that we are not living for ourselves. Again, this is the wisdom of God. They must be able to see Him in you, giving them an example of how their lives should look if they choose Him.

So again, we see that our lives are living testimonies to those who do not know Him. They should be able to see something different in your life that they do not see in others. This should provoke them to change and the number one factor should be that of love.

"But God demonstrated His own love towards us, in that while we were still sinners, Christ died for us." Romans 5:8

The word "demonstrate" is a word of action. It implies the act of doing something. Love can never be a word that we just use lightly or speak in haste. The word says that God demonstrated His love by doing something and that was sending His only Son to die for us, not while we were good or because we deserved it, but while we were still sinning.

The love that we are to have for others is the same kind of love Jesus had and still has for us. We are to love them regardless of what they are presently in, knowing that they were created with a purpose and that what they do does not determine who they are. Only the One who created them knows who they are and we have a responsibility to lead them to Him through the love in us, so that they can find out who they really are. God does not want anyone to miss the mark; not one. We have to get to the point where we too do not want to lose one soul to the enemy.

Once you begin to love as Jesus loves, you will see so many doors open up in your life to witness to God's people. God is a very jealous God when it comes to His people. He will not allow just anyone to witness to His sheep. We are seeing an emergence of New Age spiritualism taking place in our world today. People are being told that there is no physical heaven or hell, that it is within them and they are being told that God did not create us, but we create God in our own lives. The devil is a LIAR! If we are not displaying the true love of God to His people, satan can and will come in and use those ignorant of his devices to display a "false love", or a "distorted love", to draw them into his trap.

"For God so loved the world that He gave His only begotten Son, that whoever believes in Him should not perish but have everlasting life." John 3:16

It says that God loved the world, not the church, but the world, that He gave His only Son to save it, so that we could live forever with Him. The problem with the church today is that we are not going out into the world; to the lowly places to reach God's people. We have been fashioned to coming to church and being content with being saved and forgetting about everyone else who is dying in the world. Our hearts have been hardened to loving the way that God desires for us to love. Love is not selfish; love is selfless. Love gives. God could have just been thinking of Himself and chose not to sacrifice His only Son for us, but He was not selfish; He displayed the single most selfless act in history; offering His Son, so that He could gain many sons to come.

As sons of God, we should be displaying the same acts of selflessness to those who do not know Him. We have to go out into the slums, the crack houses, the strip clubs, the street corners, and anywhere that we have to go to witness the love of Jesus. If the only thing that God wanted for our lives was to save us, He would have saved us and immediately taken us to heaven. Why are we still here? We are here to be His hands and feet in the earth. Once we become transformed and restored, we have a responsibility to share what we have received with others. You have to realize that you were pulled out of satan's grip by a loving God. Now, you must have that same love within you to pull others out.

I have noticed that the church is the furthest place from people's minds that are looking for help. You would think that the church would be a safe-haven for the world to come to and feel loved and not judged, but the church has misrepresented God for generations. The church is the single most judgmental place in the world today. Instead of having banners in front of our churches that say, "All are Welcome", we have our bulletin boards or signs that say, "Baptist, Methodist, Catholic, Pentecostal, Mormon, A.M.E., Church of God in Christ", and so forth.

There is a world out there that is dying, while we are setting up our own cliques. We are not representing who we say is our Father very well. In fact, if we are not reaching out to everyone in the world without judging them, our father is not God, but the devil. Don't get angry; it is written.

*"You are of **your father** the devil, and the desires of **your father** you want to do." John 8:44 (emphasis mine)*

If you say your Father is God, then you will have the desires of your Father and I am here to let you know that God loves the world and every person in it. God does not see us in our present circumstances and determine who we are from them. No, He sees us from our created state; how He created us in the beginning. This is why God can forgive us of our sins and throw them into the sea of forgetfulness. Why is it that we are unable to love others as Jesus did? Why is it that once someone offends us or hurts us in any way, we hold onto that offense and keep not only them in bondage by not forgiving them, but keeping ourselves in bondage, because we are still holding it in our hearts?

Love is the most sacrificial act in the world. To love someone else, you must first love yourself. We are living in a world today where people are taking their own lives daily, because they feel that they are not valued. They feel that no one loves them and they have no purpose in this world, so they just think that they are doing us a favor by killing themselves. People, just letting someone know that they are loved can make all of the difference in the world. We have become a society of people who rarely even make eye contact with those that we don't know, let alone stop and speak to someone who may not "look" like us or someone who may not think like us. I have made it a point in my own day to day life to love everyone who crosses my pathway, whether it be asking how their day is going, to giving someone one of my great big hugs, to telling someone that I love them, or even just making eye contact with someone I do not know and saying hello with a smile. This is the love of God. This is the kind of love that God wants us to display to a lost and dying world.

How many of us actually do this? How many of us will take seconds out of our day to share the love of Jesus with someone? It does not take hours to plant a seed of love into someone's heart. We make it more difficult than it has to be mainly because we are either afraid of how someone is going to respond to us, or because we are ashamed to let others know that we are Believers. Love is contagious! The enemy knows this and this is why he is constantly out to destroy the core base of love in this world; the family unit. Whether it is the church family, the work family, or just a family of close friends, satan infiltrates every area of our lives, seeking to divide, so that love is disseminated, instead of being cohesive where God can cause a blessing to formulate.

Let us stop being manipulated by the enemy and learn the mind of God in the area of love. We have been raised for so long to never let our guards down; to never allow anyone to run over top of us; to get them before they get you; to do what you have to do; and to live a life that is direct opposition to the Word of God. God's love for us allows us to be who we really are. God's love produces freedom in our lives to be the very best that we can be. We do not have to always be on the defensive when someone confronts us, but we can live lives of peace knowing that the ultimate gift that we can give someone is that of love, and love is very powerful.

"And above all things have fervent love for one another, for "love will cover a multitude of sins." 1 Peter 4:8

The word fervent is defined as having or showing great warmth of feeling; intensely devoted or earnest; ardent. This word in the Greek is *ektenes*, which means intense; without ceasing. We are to possess intense love or fervent love for others and this is a love that does not cease, no matter what that person may say or do to you. This is intensely devoted love, the kind of love that God has for us. He does not stop loving us because we mess up, but He forgives us and continues to love us the same as before we messed up. You will be hurt and offended in this life by many different people, but how you respond to them will determine the outcome of not only your joy, but the way in which you share the love of God with those individuals.

I experienced a few times in my Christian walk instances where I was confronted with being led by my flesh, or by the spirit of love. It is amazing how the love of God is able to quench all of the fiery darts of the enemy. What satan wants is for you to be instantly moved by your circumstances, instead of knowing the truth and acting upon that truth, instead of your immediate feelings. I have had instances where people have been directly in my face yelling at me and because I knew what type of love God desired to offer that person, I was not moved by what was taking place in the temporal, but ultimately what would conspire out of the situation in the eternal. It is not easy if you do not know who you are in Christ. If all you are worrying about is the now and getting satisfaction out of letting someone know how you feel, you are not fit for the Kingdom of God.

Loving people takes great patience as well. Patient love says, "I am going to love you, no matter how long it takes for you to get it." It also says, "I am going to love you and not give up on you, because I feel you are not moving fast enough for me." If this were the case with God, none of us would be saved! All of us move at different paces and no one of us is the same. We must possess patience in all that we do, so that God will be glorified through the love that we are extending to His people. Are you willing to sacrifice your feelings now, so that someone can come out better later? Jesus sacrificed a great deal for us to enter into the Kingdom. What are you willing to sacrifice for someone else to enter in?

"Then He said, "Take now your son, your only son Isaac, whom you love, and go to the land of Moriah, and offer him there as a burnt offering on one of the mountains of which I shall tell you."
Genesis 22:2

What sacrifice Abraham displayed, because He knew that God not only loved him, but also Isaac. Abraham, in the Word, had no reservations about offering His son on the altar. The Word of God says that he rose up early the next morning and prepared Isaac to be sacrificed on the altar. He was sure that God would provide an offering on his behalf. As I said before, when you allow the love of God to outweigh every decision you ever make, He will open up doors of opportunity for you. He will sustain you in those difficult times and make a way for you to escape, but He does not want you to escape alone. He not only wants you, but he wants that soul that you are witnessing to as well. The love that Abraham displayed here is called patient love. He could have become impatient with God, because he was awaiting a substitute in place of his son Isaac, but instead he patiently endured even to the point of raising the knife to sacrifice his son. Now can you imagine how Isaac was feeling when he found out that he was the offering and not a lamb? Could you imagine the conversation that father and son had as Isaac lay on that altar. I am sure that Abraham told his son that he loved him, but how was Isaac to believe this if he was about to die?

Abraham surely taught Isaac in the way of the Lord and surely Isaac trusted his father as a man of wisdom. This is how others should receive you when you offer them patient love. They will know who you are and that in your patience with them; they can trust you and depend upon you in great times of need. I have experienced times in my walk with God where others trusted me totally with their lives and the lives of their children even though they were not committed to the Lord yet. They saw something in my life that bore witness to their inner man, or spirit. Even if they do not see it at first, be patient and allow God to work out the situation.

We cannot be intimidated by the way others perceive the love that we are extending to them. They most assuredly will not understand the way you love them at first, because this is not something that they are accustomed to. Most people do not say that they love members of their own immediate family, so how can we expect them to understand that a perfect stranger is telling them that they love them? This should not move you from what you know to do and that is to love them. Again, fear is a great factor in why most believers do not witness the love of Jesus to others, but we cannot allow this fear to take over our lives and water down our witness. If you say that you are a follower of Christ, then fear must not be an excuse as to why you cannot share Christ with someone.

"There is no fear in love; but perfect love casts out fear, because fear involves torment. But he who fears has not been made perfect in love." *1 John 4:18*

It says perfect love casts out fear. Perfect in this text means complete. So if the love that you are giving someone is complete, it should cast away all fear, not only in you, but also in the one whom you are extending it to. Perfect loves says, "I do not expect anything from you; I just love you." Most people cannot accept this, because they have been used to others expecting something in return for their love. When someone knows that you love them and that you do not want something in return, they can feel free to share their problems with you and not feel threatened or intimidated. There is freedom in perfect love, because it allows you to be you; no strings attached.

This is the kind of love that God extended to us when He offered salvation to us through His Son Jesus. God did not expect us to get it all right before He chose to love us and save us, even in the midst of our sinful nature. (Romans 5:8) We have not been called to judge the world, but to love them. It is not our job to judge them and it was not even Jesus' assignment to judge them. The Word says that He came not to condemn the world, but to save the world. (John 3:17) We all need to be conscious that we were all sinners and that we all still have our own issues. No one is perfect, so we do not have the right to judge anyone based upon what they are doing wrong. Let us draw others to Christ through that perfect love that is dwelling on the inside of us.

Next, we will deal with sacrificial love. Sacrifice means the act of giving up, destroying, permitting injury to, or forgoing something valued for the sake of something having a more pressing claim. When we sacrifice our time to offer love to another, we have to see it as a great investment. We cannot look at it as a burden or a bother to share the love of God with someone. Sacrificial loves says, "I do not care what I have to go through with you to get you to where you need to go." It says, "I am willing to suffer with you, in order for you to obtain the promise that God has for your life." This is powerful! Not too many people are willing to sacrifice their wants and desires for those who are in dire need of someone to talk to. It is time for us to lay down our lives for our brothers and sisters, even as Jesus laid down His life for us. The single most sacrificial act of love that has ever rocked this world was that of the sacrificial Lamb of God.

Paul was a great example of this type of love in the New Testament. The witness of this great Apostle was unmatched among the many disciples in the Bible. Paul had been transformed by the One True God on the road to Damascus and because of the great love that he found in His Father, he wanted to share with everyone that he possibly could, the love of Jesus Christ. Paul went to great extents to share the love of God with people from all over the world. He travelled extensively from city to city, sacrificing his own life many times to speak not only of the love of God, but of his own love for the people of God.

Time after time, we see in the Pauline texts where Paul is telling the different churches how much he loves them and how he would lay down his own life for them. He knew what his purpose was after being transformed on that road and because of that, he accepted his calling and his assignment. Paul knew what the true meaning of love was and he knew that it superseded his wants, desires, needs, and ultimately, his own life. The church became Paul's main focus in his life. He wanted to show them how to love one another, so that the church would prosper and grow.

"I now rejoice in my sufferings for you, and fill up in my flesh what is lacking in the afflictions of Christ, for the sake of His body, which is the church," Colossians 1:24

Paul said for the sake of His body, which is the church. Paul was not thinking of himself, but putting others' needs before his own; sacrificial love. He laid down his life for the sake of the church. He understood that his sacrifice now was for a greater cause later; for future generations of the church. This is how the church now should continue to operate. We need to pull from the vast supply of wisdom that is in the Pauline texts, so that we can live the lives of love that God purposed for us. God would not expect you to be nailed to a cross as His Son was to show your love for His people, even though there are still many today who are being martyred because of their love for God's people. God just expects you to love others with a genuine love and treat them like they should be treated.

I believe that the enemy has hardened our hearts by making us think that we cannot really make a difference in this world. We look at the global scope of disaster, destruction, and devastation and it overwhelms us to the point of believing that we cannot even begin to help others out of this darkness. The devil is a liar! Love can be offered in so many different ways and if we allow the Holy Spirit to guide and lead us, He will give us great insight and wisdom into how God desires for us to love His people.

Love is the single most important factor in healing a hurting and dying world. We can go all the way back to the beginning of time and see examples of hate that developed from the act of sin in the Garden of Eden. The story of Cain and Abel is really the first act of murder in the Bible. The two brothers had two distinctly different occupations; one was a keeper of the sheep and the other was a tiller of the ground. They both gave to the Lord an offering, but the Bible says that Abel not only brought the first fruit, but that he offered the fat also, which is representative of the finest part or richest part. God respected Abel's offering, but Cain was angry, because God did not recognize his offering.

The result of this was Cain murdering his brother Abel. Hate is the exact opposite of love and we know that there is a battle going on everyday in this world between the two. If the church cannot step up and defend love at all costs, how can a sinful world even begin to see the light at the end of the tunnel? I know that this may sound far fetched for many of you, but ignoring or not offering love to another human being is in close company to hating them. It is saying, "This is not my problem" or "I don't know them well enough to love them." The word of God makes it very simple for us.

"And the second, like it, is this: 'You shall love your neighbor as yourself.' There is no other commandment greater than these."
Mark 12:31

If you know how to love yourself, then you will be able to love those whom you don't know. If Cain would have known who he was and if he had given from his very best, then he would not have made the decision to murder his brother. We must begin to make love our top priority in this world and then we will begin to see change take place in it. We all serve a major role in the furthering of God's Kingdom in this earth. We all have a certain group of people that we will impact in this world for God. The people that you will reach, I cannot minister to. The people that God has entrusted to me; you cannot reach. He gives us all gifts to reach the people who He has predestined for us to touch. Do not allow those individuals that God has entrusted you with to slip through the cracks of this world.

You must begin to see them as your brothers and sisters. Your heart must begin to tear each and every time you see someone hurting; those on drugs, those who are homeless, those who are prostituting their bodies, those who have AIDS, those who are oppressed in other countries, those who are poor, those who are losing their homes, those who have lost their families, those who are persecuted for their faith, and so forth. There is a world out there that is awaiting a helping hand and we have to know that God cannot and will not move in the earth realm without a vessel in which He can operate through.

The church must stop pre-judging people and start loving them to Christ. No matter what it is that they are going through; no matter how wrong or bad you may think that it is, God still loves them, so why don't you? Do you realize that if you would just put aside your ideologies for a moment and begin to love someone enough to intercede for them that God might just hear you and change that person's life? You are more important in the lives of others than you think. You have a greater role in the life of another individual than you realize.

17

From the Genesis 4 text, verse 9, Cain said, "Am I my brother's keeper?" Well yes, he was supposed to be, as we are supposed to be for others.

"But concerning brotherly love you have no need that I should write to you, for you yourselves are taught by God to love one another;" 1 Thessalonians 4:9

We are all created by God and He does not love any one of us better than the other. He loves us all the same and His desire is for us to love as He loves. There are so many scriptures in the Bible that deal with love; in fact, close to five hundred separate scriptures on love are mentioned. We must assume that is was very important to God for us to catch the revelation of love. Love is the glue that knits all of humanity together. It is the chisel that breaks those hard stones into tiny little pieces; allowing humility to gain a foot hold in our lives. Love is the gentle breeze that blows across our paths at that opportune moment, giving us courage to face another day. Love is that bright light that shines in the midst of sheer darkness, illuminating even the most obscure areas of our being. However we view love, it ultimately leads us back to the One true love of our lives and that is God Himself, who loved the world so much that He allowed His Son to die, so that we would know it for ourselves.

"He who does not love does not know God, for God is love."
1 John 4:8

If you are a Believer and you profess to have Christ abiding on the inside of you, then you must love as He loves. We are to be imitators of Christ and if we know what He went through, then we will know how to love those, not only whom we do not know, but more importantly those who actually hate us or even persecute us. There were many in the days of Jesus who just outright could not stand Him. There were scholars who were offended at His wisdom, leaders who were jealous of His influence, and even family members and friends who mocked Him calling Him a mere carpenter. How did He respond to them? The way that only Jesus could; with Love.

How do you respond in the face of adversity? What is your immediate response to someone who is calling you names, threatening you, or to someone who has hurt you in any way? The response of a believer should be the same response that our great Savior would have given; Love. I have seen first hand the transformation that has taken place in a person's life who has confronted me with anger, hate, and even malice. I thank God for His Word and for His Spirit that guides me daily. We cannot in and of ourselves love in this way. We have to be taught how to love like Jesus loves. If my mind had not been transformed through the power of His Word and the power of His Spirit, I would most likely have done what many people do and that is handle it in my own way, but instead, I allowed what I had learned through His Word to come out of me, through the leading of the Holy Spirit.

In all of these instances, God proved Himself to be mighty and faithful. Did it happen overnight? No, because God is a God that desires to get the full glory out of a transformed life. I had to endure much persecution and wait on the Lord's perfect timing for His will to be done in the lives of these individuals. I could have become frustrated and given up on these precious souls, but I understood that it was not about me and how I may have felt, but that it was all about Him and what He wanted to happen in the lives of His children. Instead of allowing my flesh to rise up in opposition to them, I did what the Word of God told me to do about the situation; I loved them, blessed them, and prayed for them.

"But I say to you, love your enemies, bless those who curse you, do good to those who hate you, and pray for those who spitefully use you and persecute you." Matthew 5:44

This is powerful. We have been raised for so long to get even with anyone who may have done us wrong, but there is no freedom or liberty in this type of mindset. You continue on in this kind of behavior and the only real one that is affected by this is you. When you love someone regardless of what it is that they may have done to you, it releases the power of God into that situation to reverse it. It shows that person that you are not like others, and it will cause them to question who you are and why you respond the way you respond. And what is the ultimate goal? To lead them directly to your source; God.

In one of these instances, I was confronted by someone who really did not know me. This individual accused me of behavior that, if you are someone who knows me, is not a part of my character. I knew that this person was hurt and offended, but I knew that it was not for the reasons that they were giving me. I immediately went into intercession on behalf of this individual and the situation. God revealed to me not only the cause of it, but the true culprit behind it. I was able now to cover not only the individual, but the plot of satan to divide a church. I continued to love this person with everything that I had in me and refused to give up on them. To this day, we are able to talk about this situation as mature believers and God has allowed transformation to take place in our relationship.

When you love someone in spite of what it looks like in the natural, you are able to confuse the plans of the enemy over that situation. You are to give the enemy no room to come in and disrupt the peace of God in your life by any means. What satan wants is to disrupt the flow of love operating in the earth. He wants to divide us as much as he possibly can before we can realize the commanded blessing that lies in unity. (Psalm 133:3) For centuries, we have seen the degradation of entire races of people, because of the lack of love in our societies. From generation to generation we have been taught to stick with our own and not to associate with those who are not like us, whether by race, culture, gender, social, or economical status. Because of this, we have cut ourselves off from the very individuals that God has predestined for us to meet. It was never God's intention to separate us, but for us to live in peace and harmony; to glorify Him.

Satan has made it his priority to divide us in any and every area of our lives that he can. The entrance of sin into the world removed us from the constant communion that we were supposed to experience with our Father daily, as Adam and Eve experienced in the Garden of Eden. The love that was expressed between Creator and creation was unmatched. It says that they heard the voice of the Lord God walking in the cool of the day. But when they disobeyed God and ate of the forbidden fruit, the constant communion, or love, was lost. From that very act of disobedience; the cutting off of fellowship from God; hate entered into the world. Satan did not want to see the man that God had created live in fellowship with the Father. He was cast out of heaven, because of his vanity and pride and because of this; he did not want anyone to experience the love that he once experienced with the Father.

So from that time on, creation has battled with pride, arrogance, hatred, envy, strife, wrath, selfish ambitions, jealousy, and so much more. Satan had tampered with our thoughts for so long, that we have played into his game and lost the very essence of our being, and that is love. He maneuvers like the cunning serpent that he is and infiltrates every area of our lives, causing us to miss the whole point of our existence in the earth. We have come to the point where we barely even show love for our families, let alone someone whom we do not know. We are expected, if you will, to love our own families. You can kind of say it is "a given" to do so, but the Word of God tells us why this is not to be so.

"But if you love those who love you, what credit is that to you? For even sinners love those who love them." Luke 6:32

We have to stand out as believers. Others should look at us and see something entirely different than that of the world. The love that God desires for us to extend is designed to draw them out of the sin that entangles their lives. I am right now in a position where I have been praying and interceding for several individuals whom God has placed on my heart. It has been quite a while and I have not seen with my natural eye the manifestation of any of what I have been praying for, but because my love for them is so genuine, I refuse to give up on them. I know who I am and I know who God is in my life and I know that His Word is true and that His Spirit is leading my every move. We have to allow this love to permeate our very being. Allow His Word, which is the embodiment of who He is, to impregnate your soul. When you begin operating in the full essence of love in your life; situations, circumstances, individuals, and every thing that rises up in opposition to that love, will bow down and submit. Love is the most powerful entity in the world. It has the capacity to change people, cities, countries, nations, and yes, the entire world.

Let everything that you do be done in love. (1 Corinthians 16:14) We cannot successfully reach a lost world for Christ if we are not displaying this love within the house of the Lord first. The Word of God says that judgment will begin in the house first. (1 Peter 4:17a) Now when we read this scripture out further, it tells us that if judgment begins with us first, what will be the end of those who do not obey the gospel of God? (1 Peter 4:17b) We are to join together in unity and in love, so that we can successfully pull these precious souls out of the teeth of the enemy. I have seen so many in the body of Christ, believers or those who call themselves believers, turn their noses up at people who actually come into the house of the Lord looking for help. They pre-judge these individuals and tear them down before they can even be touched by the Holy Spirit.

The church has been misrepresented for so long. The very place where people should be able to come to and find rest and a place of safety has become an eye-sore to the world. They call us hypocrites or phonies and are finding other means of developing a spiritual existence outside of the true and living Word of God, because we are failing to epitomize who it is that we say we believe in. These other false religions are making great strides in drawing non-suspecting souls into their trap. They are displaying a tainted and clouded form of love to trick people into believing that their way is the way to bliss. Time is short saints of God and if we do not pick up our cross and begin to die daily to self, then we are going to see so many souls lost to the enemy, but there is hope. Our Father can redeem the time and will redeem the time for us if we are willing to submit and be obedient to the assignment that He has given to us. Let us allow that light to shine within the house of the Lord to strengthen the foundations of the church once again, so that we can re-open the doors of the church and allow God to be God.

"So show them your love, and prove to all the churches that our boasting about you is justified." 2 Corinthians 8:24

This is not only showing the world who we are, but again, judgment has to start in the house first. Dr. Will Moreland taught a series on "Show the House to the House"[2] and the Lord really began to speak to me about the love that He had placed on the inside of me. I always felt like I was strange. I wondered why there were not too many people within the church who were as passionate as I was about the people of God. I did not feel as if I had any true brothers or sisters that I could confide in, because I felt as if I was always being judged, even in the house of the Lord. I would get strange looks or stares, because of the way I worshipped. When I entered into prayer or intercession, I would get looks from many within the house, but this did not cause me to vacillate. I knew who I was and who God was in my life, and I knew the power of God rested and abided on the inside of me.

I had a precious woman of God speak into my life concerning this issue. She prophesied to me that I would "show the house to the house". This confounded me because again, our man of God had just ministered on this very topic. She told me that God was pleased with me and that He needed me to show His love to the church. I was overwhelmed at first, because I could not understand why God would use me to do this. I began to question myself, as I had done previously in other situations where God had spoken to me. I quickly submitted, knowing that He is God and if He said it, then I would do it. When God provides you with an assignment, the necessary tools will be readily available to you; you will not lack anything. As I began to obey His voice in several circumstances, I saw opposition rise up, but this did not move me out of my position. I knew from the beginning that this would happen, so I continued to intercede in love for my brothers and sisters, until the manifestation of God's promise unfolded in their lives.

Again, loving others as God loves them does not come automatically. We have to first find out who He is and what He did for us before we can look past others' weaknesses and love them. We need to be reminded almost daily how God brought us out of our mess. If we do not, then it is very easy to judge others for what it is that we think they are doing wrong. Again, do not judge them, but love them. It is not our job to condemn or to judge, but we are to welcome people with open arms into the fellowship of God, and let them know that they are loved and welcomed.

As you begin to understand the love of God in your own life; you will better know how to express love to others. We must humble ourselves daily and understand that our lives are not our own and that at any time, if we do not guard ourselves, we too can fall. (1 Corinthians 10:12) The kind of love that God has for us is an unconditional love, or an agape love. The word agape is defined as the love of God or Christ for humankind. A second definition that relates to us, as believers, is the love of Christians for other persons, corresponding to the love of God for humankind. So again, if you understand the love God shares towards you, then you will correspond by offering this kind of love to those who are lost and dying in this world.

"Let all that you do be done with LOVE." 1 Corinthians 16:14 (emphasis mine)

I pray that you will continue to allow the love of God to have reign and rule in your heart, so that He can effectively move through you to draw His people to Him. You are on assignment. Will you answer the call?

THE GIFT OF THE HOLY SPIRIT

"And they were all filled with the Holy Spirit, and began to speak with other tongues, as the Spirit gave them utterance."

Acts 2:4

As a child, I attended our family church, which was right directly up the street from our home. We attended Sunday school regularly and then proceeded into the main sanctuary for church services. All of this was very normal to me; it was just something that we did. I never remembered asking Jesus into my heart, but I do remember always being there on Sunday.

Time progressed and my father moved us away from this church to one that seemed at first very strange to me; even scary. First of all, the United Methodist Church that I grew up in was very quiet in their worship and very reserved. If we did sing a song of praise, it still had the air of worship to it. This new church was very loud and they played all sorts of instruments. This was so very new to me, being that I only remember singing to the tune of a church organ.

I began to feel comfortable, because the songs were nice and everyone just seemed so happy, as opposed to seeing faces with not much expression at all for years. We began to enter into worship, and all of a sudden people began to cry out in other languages. It frightened me at first, because no one ever did this at my family's church. I looked around and *everyone* was doing this.

> *"For they heard them speak with tongues and magnify God..."*
> Acts 10:46

My father had been diagnosed with cancer and heard from the Lord to leave our family's church. I remember the very day that I saw him leave his chair and walk down the aisle to the altar. Tears were rolling down his face and I had no idea what he was even doing? The only reason that I ever remember going to the altar as a child was for Communion, and I did not see any bread or juice at that altar. I remember crying, because I saw him crying, which was something that I was not accustomed to seeing him do. Again, the people began to pray in another language and I was frustrated, because I did not know what they were saying. My father is at the altar with the Pastor's hand on his chest and the other one on his head and everyone is getting louder and louder, as they are praying in this language.

Not too long after this, during Vacation Bible School, I was also led into my prayer of salvation. I was about twelve years of age and I remember feeling like I had really just started going to church. It was fun and everyone seemed happy. My father really began to study the Word of God and things seemed to be getting much better. Two years later, my father passed away. I was devastated to say the least and I did not attend church any longer, because no one else in my family attended church. Needless to say, I did not return to the Lord, until I was twenty-two years old. I began to grow and learn things about God that I had not known before. I began experiencing things that I had not previously experienced when it came to church. This was eight years from the time that I stopped going to church; representing 'new beginnings'.

I received the gift of the Holy Spirit in January of 2003, exactly seven years from the date of me returning to the Lord, and my life has never been the same since. I became so strengthened within myself and saw my walk with the Lord skyrocket. I felt myself being built up on the inside and I knew that it was because of the evidence of speaking in unknown tongues.

"He who speaks in a tongue edifies himself, but he who prophesies edifies the church." 1 Corinthians 14:4

The Lord began to open my 'spiritual eyes'. I began to pray so differently than I had previously. I prayed a lot, but I never knew how ineffective my prayers had been until this point. He (the Holy Spirit) would ask me to pray for people, but not give me specifics of what to even pray for. He would just tell me to get up and pray. I did this for several months nearly every night and my faith began to increase and my walk with the Lord went to another level. Even though I did not "see" the results of my prayers, I trusted God as I had never trusted Him before.

I knew it was Him who was waking me up to pray, because I never used to wake up in the early morning hours. I was one of those 'deep sleepers', but this was occurring on a regular basis and I enjoyed spending time in the presence of the Lord. This occurred one night in November of 2003. I had only been in Germany for about seven months, but in this time, I was being built up tremendously in my spirit. The Lord awakened me and told me to go into my son's room and pray. He, the Holy Spirit, told me to pray for some friends of mine and my husband's who had been stationed with us at a previous military duty station. I did not know what to pray for specifically, so I just covered their marriage, health, and family. I spoke and prayed in my heavenly tongue, and did so until the peace of God filled my heart.

I knew that they were stationed in a nearby country, but I did not know how to contact them. I had my friends' mother's phone number and decided to call her to get her daughter's contact information to see how they were doing. The phone number that I had dialed was disconnected. I just assumed that I would probably never hear from them again. In January of the following year, the Holy Spirit quickened me to try the number again, so I obeyed.

My friend Jenny's brother answered the phone and told me that they were still in Italy and proceeded to give me her phone number. He hesitated and asked me if I knew what had happened to her husband Kenny? I told him no with a huge knot in my throat, and he explained to me that he had been deployed to Iraq and that his convoy had been hit by a roadside bomb. My heart began to race, because I already knew in my spirit that God had intervened in this man's life. I contacted her and she began to explain to me all that had taken place in Iraq. I pondered adding this story to the book, but the Holy Spirit shared with me that it was vital to the effectiveness of this message. This story is told in his own words:

(Excerpt from e-mail dated November 1, 2007)

13 Nov 2003, around 15:00 hrs. I was on a convoy from Balad to Tikrit, about 30-40 miles out. I was on a 40 pack bus full of soldiers on the deadly (IED ROAD), then bam, I heard this loud boom and in slow motion, I see dirt, glass, and fire all around me. I can feel the pain from the dirt and glass on my face and feel the fire's heat all over my body, but all in slow motion Debbie, and once I could see the soldier in front of me, half of his right shoulder and neck were half gone and from his knee down was gone. Then things went back to regular speed and everyone was jumping out of windows and just trying to get the hell off of the bus before they hit it with an RPG. So, I grabbed Fletcher and ran off the bus on top of this hill and got a medic there and all the while, there is enemy fire coming from our rear flank. I lost it and began running after three Iraqi's and shot them. One of my soldiers, Pierre, came and caught me from falling and said, "SSG Hill, you are hit!" I looked at my left side and saw my entire lower left side covered in blood and a big 5 inch hole. I remember pushing my soldiers away from me and then, I woke up in the hospital two days later, getting ready to have a six hour long surgery.

The Gift of the Holy Spirit

(Excerpt from e-mail dated November 2, 2007)

Let me tell you this, when I got blown up, two days later, the chaplain and Rear D Commander came to my home in Italy and told Jenny I was dead. I have the e-mail where they listed me DOA. So I am blessed. So thank you for your prayers, your kind heart, and your ability to believe and act on it when the Lord speaks to you because that night, if you had not have listened to your instincts and prayed for me, I may not be here.

Retired SSG Kenneth Hill,
Stuttgart, Arkansas
Veteran/Operation Iraqi Freedom

This e-mail resounded in my spirit for days. Our capacity to hear from the Holy Spirit could be the difference between life and death for someone. Remember Lot and his family? Abraham interceded for them and God spared their lives. Today, Kenny is walking when the doctors told him that he would be paralyzed from the waist down, and as you read in his e-mail excerpt, they had declared him dead. Oh, the devil is a liar! Whose report are we going to believe? He and his wife, not too long after this ordeal, gave birth to a beautiful baby boy. Glory to God! God had a plan for this man's life and satan knew that very well, but God stepped in and turned it around for His glory! In the excerpt you heard him say that if I had not listened to "my instincts", but I am here to tell you all that it was not mere instincts, but the Omnipotent, Omniscient, and Omnipresent third person of the Godhead; the Holy Spirit. Our spirits are not limited, as is our natural bodies. We cannot physically be in more than one place at any given time, but our spirits can travel great distances, as we move in the realm of intercession.

The gift of the Holy Spirit is very essential to intercession. One has to be willing and able to "hear" what the Spirit is saying. There may be instances during your day when the Spirit will 'prompt' you to pray for someone. This 'prompting' is the ear of your inner man, or spirit. Many of us, including myself at one time, play this off as coincidence and do not act upon the prompting, because we are not spiritually grounded. If you are able to hear and have received the gift of the Holy Spirit, do not brush this off as just mere coincidence. We must be willing and obedient to act upon what we hear and pray immediately, even if we are not given specifics to intercede for at that time. We, in and of ourselves, are limited, but the Spirit of God will help us.

"Likewise the Spirit also helps in our weaknesses. For we do not know what we should pray for as we ought, but the Spirit Himself makes intercession for us with groanings which cannot be uttered." *Romans 8:26*

We must not waste time trying to 'figure out' what to pray, but move out immediately and trust the Holy Spirit that He knows what He is doing. I believe that the biggest problem that intercessors face is thinking too much and not allowing the Holy Spirit to lead. I myself used to get so anxious, because I wanted to know more, so that I could effectively pray, but God showed me through the last example of intercession that all I had to do was "hear", be obedient, and to intercede when He prompted me. Glory to God!

Another thing that an intercessor must realize is that they are not the one who has carried the miracle out, but God Himself. God cannot move in the earth realm without a vessel. God only moves through those who are willing and obedient. It is a great privilege to be used by God in such a way, but we must remember that all of the glory goes to God and God alone. I spoke earlier about speaking in our heavenly language or "tongue". What this does is builds up or edifies our spirit. As you develop your tongue, you become more confident in the Spirit of God and you will be able to better discern what it is that you are hearing from the Holy Spirit.

The word "discern" is defined as to perceive by the sight or some other sense or by the intellect; see, recognize, or apprehend. This word in the Hebrew is *yada*, which means to know. Even though these two definitions imply the same meaning, there is a difference between seeing and knowing. *"For we walk by faith and not by sight."* (2

Corinthians 5:7) God desires for us to know in our spirit when He speaks to us. We have to have confidence in Who it is that we are hearing from; therefore, giving us boldness to enter into intercession. We should not have to see something or hear a specific word to know what to pray for. We, in faith, believe that the Holy Spirit is leading and guiding our every word; therefore, we move and obey and allow Him to do the rest.

Now this does not mean that we should only intercede if we hear specifically from God to do so, but we should at all times stay in an atmosphere of intercession. Those who intercede have an air about them that is noticeable. They are always watching and guarding in the spirit. Everything they see and hear is automatically transferred into the spiritual to see what God is saying about the situation. They are always led by the Spirit of God and even though you may not physically see them praying; they are.

"Therefore I exhort first of all that supplications, prayers, intercessions, and giving of thanks be made for all men." 1Timothy 2:1

Once this becomes a lifestyle for you, God will begin to speak specific instructions into your prayer life. He will have seen your obedience, commitment, and faithfulness in this area and begin to trust you to intercede for great situations. Again, it is not about being worthy of such a gift, but because of your willingness and obedience; being that He is the only worthy One.

Keep this in mind; you have to first "accept" this responsibility. It is not required, because God does not force any of us to pray or intercede, but once you make the choice to accept the call, you are held to a greater level of responsibility. I found through my experience that even when I felt overwhelmed and just wanted God to stop speaking to me; my spirit longed to hear from Him, and I could not let go of the fulfillment I felt as I entered into the presence of the Lord in intercession.

Many in the body of Christ do not accept the infilling of the Holy Spirit to be something of importance or even something that is for everyone, but the Word of God specifically uses the triumvirate body of Father, Son, and Holy Spirit continually throughout the Bible. Why would it be mentioned if it were not paramount to our Christian growth? How can we accept one without the other? We cannot, because they are not separate; but One. When Jesus ascended to heaven, He told His disciples to wait for the promise of God, which was the infilling of the Holy Spirit of God.

"And being assembled together with them, He commanded them not to depart from Jerusalem, but to wait for the Promise of the Father, "which," He said, "you have heard from Me;" Acts 1:4

This specific command was of vital importance to Jesus. He would not have commanded the disciples to stay and wait for this gift before they departed on their journey if it were not paramount to His message. He advised them that their receiving the baptism of water from John was necessary, but that there was a greater baptism that was coming and that they should wait for it if they were to be effective witnesses for Him in the earth. Again, nothing that we do in and of ourselves in this earth will benefit the Kingdom of God. It is only through the word of God and the power of His Spirit that we can accomplish anything for Him.

The Spirit of the Living God was given to us by God as a gift. He could have left us here without any help, but He loves us so very much that He desires to have a way to communicate with those whom He created. The word of God says that He will never leave us nor forsake us. (Hebrews 13:5) So when Jesus was taken up, He advised them not to make any decisions until they received the promise from God their Father, which was the Holy Spirit. That promise was fulfilled not many days after that. Over one hundred and twenty disciples stood together in what we call "The Upper Room". They continued together in steadfast prayer until the Spirit of God entered the room.

"And suddenly there came a sound from heaven, as of a rushing mighty wind, and it filled the whole house where they were sitting. Then there appeared to them divided tongues, as of fire, and one sat

upon each of them. And they were all filled with the Holy Spirit and begun to speak with other tongues, as the Spirit gave them utterance."
Acts 2:2-4

There are many who say that they are filled with the Holy Spirit, but who do not recognize the tongue as the initial evidence of receiving this gift. The tongue is known as our heavenly language. This is the way that God chose to communicate with us in the earth after the ascension of His Son Jesus. The church has marked this gift a taboo, if you will, and now even people who call themselves Christians think that this is evidence of cult activity. The devil is a liar. This was the initial evidence of the church being formed in the earth. We saw in Acts that all one hundred and twenty disciples believed that what Jesus told them would come; would come, and they stood in expectation of receiving this gift.

We see immediately in the scriptures that after the outpouring of the Holy Spirit, there were many souls being added to the church, as well as multiple healings taking place. The power that came along with the gift of the Holy Spirit enabled the disciples to carry out God's will in the lives of His people. As an intercessor, the gift of the Holy Spirit is absolutely necessary to carry out God's plan in this earth. If you have not received the gift of the Holy Spirit, then I encourage you to do so. Having a desire to intercede for the nations is noble, but you cannot do this in your own power. There has to be a divine connection taking place between heaven and earth. Heaven's agenda has to enter the earth realm and it can only enter into the earth realm through the original form of communication, and that is the Holy Spirit.

The many revivals that took place in the world were evidence of the outpouring of the Holy Spirit; from generation to generation, we saw people accepting that great gift of God's Spirit into their lives and the entire atmosphere of their community changed. We cannot lose sight of this very important aspect of our Christian walk. When we do, we will see church as usual; people in the church still living in sin; frustrated, angry, and living any kind of way. The Spirit of God cannot and will not operate in such an environment. Where there is no power, people will stay the same; where there is no power, souls will not be delivered; where there is no power, signs, wonder, and miracles will not take place. There has to be a revival of the outpouring of the Holy Spirit in this earth for God to begin to move on behalf of His people.

Whether it begins with entire congregations, or just one submitted, committed, and obedient vessel, God's plans can and will succeed in this hour. You have to be willing to be set apart from the rest and willing to suffer persecution if you are going to be used by God in the area of intercession. People will call you crazy and some may even stir up controversy about you, but you cannot be moved by their ignorance. You must know who you are and Whose you are and stand your post as an intercessor. If Jesus Himself had to be filled with the Holy Spirit, why are we not also supposed to be filled?

"Then Jesus, being filled with the Holy Spirit, returned from the Jordan and was led by the Spirit into the wilderness," Luke 4:1

Once you are filled the Holy Spirit there will be a time of testing for you. The word says that immediately after being filled, Jesus was led by the Spirit into the wilderness. This is a time of teaching and impartation for the intercessor. This is where you will begin to understand how to receive from the Spirit's leading. This will also be a time of finding out how satan maneuvers; what tactics, schemes, and plots he uses to distract the intercessor. The word reveals three separate times that satan took Jesus up to tempt Him, but each time Jesus gave him the Word of God. This is why it is important for us to know the Word of God because satan himself knows the word. If you cannot come with the word, he is going to tear you to pieces in the realm of the spirit.

As an intercessor, you have to be on the offensive at all times. You cannot let your guard down thinking that you are standing on solid ground and that nothing can happen to you. I found out several years after I began operating in the ministry of intercession that satan wanted to take me out. He knew that I was effectively operating in the gift of the Holy Spirit and that results were manifesting through my obedience to the Spirit's leading. I felt myself becoming easily distracted and I even found it hard to hear the Holy Spirit's voice prompting me to intercede. I became very tired and I always found myself sitting down and immediately falling asleep. I recognized it as an attack from the enemy because he knew the hour of my assignment. He knew that every morning at 3:00am, the Holy Spirit would awaken me to intercede.

I had to gain my composure and throw myself even the more into the Word of God and into the presence of God. As an intercessor, you must be ready to be attacked by the enemy. You must be prepared, as I said earlier, to discern when satan is out to steal those precious times of fellowship with the Holy Spirit. You will read in the following chapters ways to combat the enemy's tactics on your life; how to guard against his cunning manipulations to keep you from hearing from the Holy Spirit.

I believe that this was the greatest test of my walk with God. In the midst of it, I found myself very vulnerable, but I still felt the presence of God covering me. I still heard His voice, even though it became very faint at one point. I found myself battling to stay awake to meet with Him; my flesh continued to rise up in opposition to my spirit. I would cry at times because I felt as if I was being disobedient to the call, but the Holy Spirit would always come to comfort me and guide me right back into the presence of God. The Holy Spirit is also referred to as the Comforter in the Word of God.

"And I will pray the Father, and he shall give you another Comforter, that he may abide with you for ever;" John 14:16, KJV

The Holy Spirit is there to comfort us in our greatest times of need, especially as an intercessor. God understands the sacrifice that intercessors embark upon as they enter into the realm of the spirit on behalf of people and situations. He also understands the attacks that will take place in the life of an intercessor, so He allows the Comforter, or the Holy Spirit, to come in and restore to them the necessary strength to continue on in their assignment. This experience drew me even closer to the Father, knowing that when He provided the assignment; He provided everything that I needed to carry out the assignment. This is something that intercessors should keep at the forefront of their minds. God will not allow you to be left out there alone, but He always provides a way for you to accomplish what He desires.

The Holy Spirit should be to you like water is to a fish. Most fish can only remain alive outside of water for a short span of time; some a few hours, but the majority will die if they are not placed back in the water. This is how the intercessor should feel without the presence of the Holy Spirit. I remember how I was before I received the gift of the Holy Spirit. I was saved, but I knew that there was something missing from this experience. I thought when I got saved that everything would fall into place and I would begin to walk with God in mighty ways. I read the Word of God daily and I prayed as most Christians did, but I could not grasp why I was not experiencing the kinds of things that the disciples in the Bible experienced? It was not until I received the gift of the Holy Spirit that I saw my walk with the Lord soar. My prayer life changed dramatically and my strength grew greatly. I caught a hold of God's will for my life and I began to walk in the very gifting that was created in me. It was not until I experienced the attack from satan, that I realized how important the Holy Spirit was in my life. David, in the Psalms, sends a resounding statement that solidifies how important the Holy Spirit is in the life of an intercessor.

"Do not cast me away from Your presence, And do not take Your Holy Spirit from me." Psalm 51:11

David knew that without the Holy Spirit in his life; God's never ending communion with His children; he was nothing. He knew that his spiritual life, as well as his natural life, depended upon the leading and guiding of the Holy Spirit. This became a great reality in my life as well. I felt as if I were dying during these moments of testing for me. I felt as if I was sinking into a depression that I was not going to come out of. I walked around lost for days because I felt like I missed the mark, but the Holy Spirit was right there to help me get back on track. It is very important to know that you can do nothing without the help of the Holy Spirit as an intercessor. If this can become a reality to you, then you will not feel overwhelmed when you miss the mark. Just get back up and get back into position. He will lead you right back to the point where you left off.

Another important thing to know as an intercessor is to not place more responsibility on yourself than is expected of you. You are not God, so you do not have to worry yourself with things that are not yours to worry about. The assignment of an intercessor is to first obey, then to hear from the Holy Spirit, and to intercede. After this, it is no longer your assignment. All God needs is a willing and obedient vessel to act upon His word and release it into the earth realm. After this, He is done. We have to know that it was already finished on the cross, so the victory in every situation that you intercede upon is already yours. Just open your mouth and speak. The Holy Spirit will give you the very words that you will need to say. You do not have to think or rationalize about what to say or do; just say what you hear.

"But when they arrest you and deliver you up, do not worry beforehand, or premeditate what you will speak. But whatever is given you in that hour, speak that; for it is not you who speak, but the Holy Spirit." Mark 13:11

If you are in constant fellowship with the Father through His Holy Spirit, you will receive pinpoint instructions in every area of your life. Every aspect of my day is given up to the Holy Spirit's leading. When I wake up in the morning, I make it a point to recognize the Holy Spirit and get my daily instructions from Him. I acknowledge Him as the One who guides and leads my every word, action, and footstep. I do not count any situation or circumstance as mere coincidence, but I know that the Holy Spirit leads my every move. When I see a situation occur that does not flow with what "the world" would see as normal, I understand that the Holy Spirit is moving in that situation and I react accordingly. This happens literally every day for me. I see the Holy Spirit intervene in my life consistently. Why? Because I give Him His office space. I acknowledge that not only do I have a job, but He does as well, and I purpose to always allow Him to do what He needs to do and try my best not to interfere with His assignment, as I am learning from Him what my assignment is.

It is an awesome experience to be led by the Spirit of God. It is a relationship like none other. The Holy Spirit's job is to provide insight, illumination, and revelation into the life of a believer. Insight is defined as the capacity to discern the true nature of a situation; penetration. The Holy Spirit will give you inside information into a situation that others will not see. While others are battling and debating over their take on a certain situation, you will have insight into the true nature of it and this allows you to intercede effectively. Daniel is a great example of someone who received great insight from the Spirit of God. He received through dreams and visions, insight into people's lives and was able to interpret to them their own dreams, allowing them the opportunity to turn their lives around. Now when you receive insight through intercession, the Holy Spirit will begin to show you certain things about people or situations, but it is not for you to release it, but for you to cover it in intercession. Daniel was a prophet and because of this, the insight he received was to be released to the people for their benefit. In the area of intercession, you are standing in the gap for that particular person or situation. You are to continue interceding about what you received until the Holy Spirit releases more.

Illumination is defined as to enlighten intellectually or spiritually; enable to understand. The Greek word for this is *photizo* which means to shed rays, to brighten up, enlighten, or to make to see. We get the word photo or photograph from this word. In times past, we used Polaroid cameras that would take the picture, but it would not immediately be made known to us what it looked like. It would take a little while for the image to become illuminated for us to see the true nature of the photo. This is a greater level than insight because insight just gives you the knowledge of a situation, where illumination will allow you to 'see', if you will, into the situation through understanding. When the Holy Spirit gives you insight, you take what you have received and even though you may know the true nature of it, you are still limited in how you intercede because the Holy Spirit had not allowed you to 'see' greater into the situation. Once God sees that you are faithful to intercede by just receiving insight; He will open up, or shed rays of light deeper into what He has already shown you.

Revelation is defined as communication of knowledge to man by a divine or supernatural agency; something revealed, especially a dramatic disclosure of something not previously known or realized. Revelation is the one hundred fold dimension of knowledge released by God through His Holy Spirit. As you saw in the definition, revelation reveals previously unknown information, usually in a dramatic instance. You can be interceding for a situation and immediately the Holy Spirit will send revelation into it and allow you to hit the target. The Word of God speaks of Peter receiving a revelation from God concerning the deity of Jesus.

13 When Jesus came into the region of Caesarea Philippi, He asked His disciples, saying, "Who do men say that I, the Son of Man, am?"

14 So they said, "Some say John the Baptist, some Elijah, and others Jeremiah or one of the prophets."

15 He said to them, "But who do you say that I am?"

16 Simon Peter answered and said, "You are the Christ, the Son of the living God."

17 Jesus answered and said to him, "Blessed are you, Simon Bar-Jonah, for flesh and blood has not revealed this to you, but My Father who is in heaven. Matthew 16:13-17

Revealed in this text, means to take off the cover. God took the cover off of Peter's eyes and allowed him to see Jesus for who He was. As you move in intercession, the Holy Spirit will begin to pull the cover back off of many situations that you will be interceding for and give you great revelation into it. God's purpose in intercession is to expose the forces of darkness operating in the earth realm, so as to send His light into these situations to bring deliverance. God cannot reveal these things to an individual who is not submitted. When you yield yourself to the Holy Spirit, He will begin to share many things with you. God knows the heart of an intercessor. He knows that what is on His heart is on your heart as well and because of this, He knows that He can trust you to carry out His will in the earth.

The Holy Spirit is our comforter, our helper, and our guide; the One who leads us; the One who sends insight, illumination, and revelation into our most difficult situations. Why are we not utilizing this help? Why are we not accepting this most gracious gift left here for us by our Father? One of the main reasons why people refuse to accept the gift of the Holy Spirit is because they do not want to be held accountable for what they are doing. As an intercessor, the Holy Spirit is your covering. If you are in constant fellowship with the Holy Spirit, He will prompt you when you are going in the wrong direction. Your awareness of sin becomes even the more magnified as you develop in the ministry of intercession. The time that you spend in the presence of God through His Holy Spirit causes you to develop greater hearing and greater eyesight into the spiritual realm and because of this, the natural will begin to look very different to you.

The things that you took for granted before will now seem more important and pressing to you. Others will think that you are crazy or that you are taking things to seriously, but you are developing a mind that is in direct communication with the Father through His Holy Spirit. Many will not understand you and many will even dislike you because of your relationship and communion with the Father, but you must not allow this to distract you. You are on an assignment and part of your assignment is to be a light to others who are struggling in their own assignments. I have encountered more times than I can remember people coming to me and thanking me for my relationship with God. This may sound strange, but when you are consistent in your fellowship with the Holy Spirit, others are watching you. Even if they have not yet committed to being faithful, they need to see some-one who is, so that when they are ready, they will come to you for accountability. Many times in your walk, you will be that "holy spirit" for someone else. I am not saying that you are the Holy Spirit, but you should have enough of Him on the inside of you to impart into some-one else's life when they need it. In your faithfulness and obedience, you will draw them into the presence of God.

I had a beautiful sister in the Lord, God rest her soul, who was quickened in her spirit almost every time that we spoke. She recognized my relationship with the Holy Spirit and she knew that each time that she spoke to me; she would receive from the Spirit through me, as I did from her. She would say to me, "Your spirit screams faithfulness!" She would tell me so often that when she felt as if she was getting off track that I somehow would call her or e-mail her right on time. Now this statement is not to give us any entryway to pride because the only glory goes to God, but what it is to reveal is that our walk with the Lord should show, not only in word, but in deed. Others should recognize that you are led by the Spirit of God.

"Belteshazzar, chief of the magicians, because I know that the Spirit of the Holy God is in you," Daniel 4:9a

King Nebuchadnezzar not only knew, but he saw that the Spirit of God rested upon Daniel. He was convinced through Daniel's experience and through his walk with the Lord that it was genuine and that God spoke through Daniel. Others should be convinced of your walk with the Lord and not only know that you are led by the Spirit of God, but they should be able to see it in your daily life. The enemy understands your commitment to God to intercede and because of this; he will try whatever he can to discredit your name. Always stay alert and aware spiritually through constant communion with the Holy Spirit, so that you will know when to guard yourself against his attacks.

I cannot communicate enough to you how crucial the Holy Spirit is in the life of an intercessor. Not only does He reveal things to you about others' situations, but He will reveal to you when satan tries to hinder you from interceding. Your ministry is very detrimental to the enemy's plans and he knows this, so he will pull together whatever arsenal that he has against you to try and stop you, but stand firm in the power of the Holy Spirit and know that he can do nothing if you know who you are. The Word of God says that he walks about like a roaring lion, seeking whom he may devour. (1 Peter 5:8) He does not know who he can devour, but if you let your guard down, his antenna pinpoints your location to him and now he knows what areas you are weak in and now he has a crack to enter into. Know who you are and trust in the Holy Spirit's leading and you will effectively carry out your assignment for the Lord.

He is our helper as I mentioned earlier. God desires for us to call on the help of the Holy Spirit any time that we need Him. If we do not utilize the wisdom of the Spirit of God, He cannot fulfill His assignment for God. His hands are tied if we do not access His power in the earth realm. When I went through that season of testing, I could feel the emptiness inside of me. I knew that the help of the Holy Spirit was vital to my walk with God. I understood that without Him, I was lost. I realized that once I changed partners, there was no going back for me. I knew at that point, that I served only one Master and that my life would never be fulfilled outside of the will of God.

We must be sold out to the will of God and allow His Spirit to direct our every thought, our every word, and our every footstep. When you allow this, the Spirit of God will stand for you in every area of your life. The Holy Spirit's direction will lead you away from any hurt, harm, or danger that tries to approach you. I have a co-worker that got into a terrible accident. He explained to me that his car flipped down the highway and he actually showed me the pictures of his car. Looking at it, there was no "natural" reason why he should have made it out. I was led by the Spirit of God to ask him if he remembered saying anything while he was being thrown down that highway or if there was anything different about that day than any other day. He told me that he always takes the same route to work. That day he told me that he took a new route, but something was telling him not to. I spoke to him and let him know that this was not coincidence or happenstance, but that it was merely the Holy Spirit of God prompting him of impending danger. I know that there was someone interceding for him that day and because of their faithfulness, he is here today to give his testimony.

The power of the Holy Spirit is so very real and it is a sad reality that many in the body of Christ don't believe in Him. We miss the very benefits of being a child of God. How can we believe that He loves us enough to save us, but not believe that He sent us His Spirit to watch over us and protect us? I explained to this precious young man that God was calling him and that it was not mere luck that he was saved, but the Holy One, God the Father, intervened in his life that very day. We have to have our spiritual ears open at all times to hear the very instructions that are coming not only daily, but every moment of the day. He is Omnipresent; everywhere at all times, so it does not matter where you go; He is watching over you.

There are times when I know that He is near to me. I see myself take a different route here or He will lead me to take a day off from work and then I will come across the path of someone who He needs me to minister to. He will lead someone into my office that I need to see to get an answer that I have asked God to reveal to me. I may be interceding for someone and He will somehow allow our paths to cross for a moment to impart His wisdom. I see Him everywhere. I see Him in the trees, I see Him in the water, I see Him in the sky, I see Him in the wind, but most of all for me; I see Him in the birds of the air. Just as I said before, the things that God would have you say, people will think that you are crazy or that you have lost your mind, but the relationship that I have with my Father is real.

I make it a point before I go anywhere in my car to ask the Holy Spirit to watch over me and protect me. I ask Him to guide the wheels of my vehicle completely according to His wisdom. I ask Him to divert any other vehicle that may be reckless away from my car and to send forth my angels that are encamped about me to sniff out any plot, ploy, plan, and scheme of the enemy to hinder me from getting to my destinations safely. Do I believe that this works? I absolutely do! Why do you think Psalm 91 exists in the Word of God? This chapter deals not only with confession, but declaring the word of God to be true over my life and acknowledging the Holy Spirit's part in it all. There is a partnership taking place between you and God through His Spirit. You are agreeing with His word by way of His Spirit. Glory to God! Catch a hold of this revelation. By you agreeing with His Word (Jesus) by way of His Holy Spirit, (Who was the Promise left for us) God cannot help but act on your behalf in the earth realm, because you have recognized His order; the Godhead.

I teach my children how important it is to recognize the Godhead. My son wakes up every morning and says good morning God, good morning Jesus, and good morning Holy Spirit. I have taught my children the significance of every aspect of the Godhead and why you cannot choose to ignore any part of their triumvirate existence. Many people believe in God or some form of a god. They believe that somewhere out there is the existence of a higher being. Some accept Jesus as the Son God and that He died on the cross for our sins and that because we confess our sins and accept Him, we will one day see Him in heaven. But I am here to tell you there is a vast majority of people who do not in any way recognize the Holy Spirit in their lives. They call Him their conscious, their instinct, their inner witness, their inner man, and so forth, but fail to recognize Him as He is; the Holy Spirit of God Himself living and breathing on the inside of us.

The enemy would love nothing more than to have us ignorant of this truth to the very day that we die. He understands that if we catch the revelation of the Holy Spirit in our lives that we will begin to scatter his strongholds in the earth realm. We have got to stop allowing him to deceive us saints of God. If we accept one aspect of the Word of God, then we must accept it all! You cannot pick and choose what you want to believe and leave the rest up for speculation. The word of God says that "all Scripture is inspired by God and is useful to teach us what is true and to make us realize what is wrong in our lives. It corrects us when we are wrong and teaches us to do what is right." (2 Timothy 3:16, NLT)

It says that ALL scripture is inspired by God. How do you think it came? Yes, by the Spirit of God through the disciples and apostles. They wrote as they were inspired by the Holy Spirit to write. They all received the gift of the Holy Spirit. They were among the one hundred and twenty in the upper room who received the infilling of the Holy Spirit. So we understand from these scriptures that when one receives the infilling of the Holy Spirit, God will speak great and unknown things to him through Him. We are asking God daily to reveal His will for our lives and to answer our prayers, but we are failing to recognize a vital part of Him and that is His Holy Spirit.

If we fail to accept this important aspect of God into our lives, then we will not be able to carry out His perfect will in the earth. If we fail to recognize the Holy Spirit as a vital part of our existence in this earth, then we are going to miss out on intimate communion with the

Father that can only come through His Spirit. If we fail to exercise the free gift given to us by God, then we will not be able to accomplish the assignment that He had predestined for our lives. The people whom God has in your life need an example of Him to imitate. You should be that light in the midst of darkness for them. Allow them to see God through you and allow His Holy Spirit to guide you and lead you in the way you should go.

"clearly you are an epistle of Christ, ministered by us, written not with ink but by the Spirit of the living God, not on tablets of stone but on tablets of flesh, that is, of the heart." 2 Corinthians 3:3

The Holy Spirit has to become a part of your everyday existence. He has to become your lifeline to the Father. You cannot just merely say you have received this gift and not operate in the full power of the gift. It has to sink deep into your spirit and not remain on the surface level. There is so much that God desires to do through you as an intercessor. He wants to speak His mysteries to you; He wants to reveal His plans to you; He wants to move through you; He wants to use you for His glory. Will you accept the assignment? The Word of God in John tells us clearly that if we do not accept the baptism of water and of the Spirit, we will not enter God's Kingdom.

"Jesus said, "You're not listening. Let me say it again. Unless a person submits to this original creation—the 'wind-hovering-over-the-water' creation, the invisible moving the visible, a baptism into a new life—it's not possible to enter God's kingdom. When you look at a baby, it's just that: a body you can look at and touch. But the person who takes shape within is formed by something you can't see and touch—the Spirit—and becomes a living spirit." John 3:5-6 (MSG)

Let us not be afraid any longer of receiving the infilling of the Holy Spirit. What God originally intended as a gift for us has been misconstrued as insanity? I am here to tell you firsthand that the Holy Spirit is real and that my life has been forever changed by His presence in my everyday goings and comings. I have not only been built up in my walk with the Lord, but He has used me to intercede and to intercept the plans of satan not only in my own life, but in the lives of others. Allow Him to use you for His glory.

Again, we are all called to intercede, but there is a higher level of intercession that can only be obtained through a deeper communion with the Holy Spirit and a willingness to serve God in this area. Will you answer the call?

"LOOSE LIPS SINK SHIPS"

"A time to tear, And a time to sew; A time to keep silence, And a time to speak."

Ecclesiastes 3:7

Now that you know you have been faithful in the area of intercession and you know that you are hearing from the Holy Spirit; you have to guard yourself against prematurely releasing information that God has not told you to release. "To everything there is a season, A time for every purpose under heaven." Ecclesiastes 3:1 There is a time and a season for everything and you should know if the Holy Spirit is saying, "Speak now" or if He is saying, "Be quiet and wait." This is so very crucial because you could share something with someone and hinder them greatly. You have to be able to discern what your role in the situation is. It is possible that all God wants you to do is pray and intercede and you will never hear anything else about that particular situation again.

A great mistake would be to try and force the issue and 'gain knowledge' that the Holy Spirit has not shared with you to validate that you heard from God. This is pride and we know that God abhors pride and will not commune with someone who is operating in it. So, if you continue on this pathway and say that God is speaking to you; you are operating in rebellion because God is not in it.

Please remember that it is not about you. We have to humble ourselves in the sight of God, so that He is able to use us. "God resists the proud, But gives grace to the humble." (1Peter 5:5b) As you become more intimate with God, He does begin to speak to you through His Holy Spirit. The more time you spend in His presence, the more He will reveal to you. When I first really began to pray for people and situations, God would open so many doors in my prayer life. I had such joy when I prayed, as well as peace. I could enter into His presence almost immediately and just stay there fellowshipping with Him.

After I was "called out" to intercede in a greater level, this is when my prayer life drastically changed. I felt vulnerable in a sense because I did not even know the difference between prayer and intercession. I thought that they were the same. Prayer is the direct line of communication between you and the Father in Jesus' name. This is usually intimate and personal time that you spend in His presence concerning you and your immediate family and situations. Intercession, on the other hand, usually extends outside of your personal sphere into the lives and situations of others on a deeper level.

"I exhort therefore, that, first of all, supplications, prayers, intercessions, and giving of thanks, be made for all men." 1Timothy 2:1, KJV

So we see here that prayer and intercession are distinctly categorized. Prayer in this text is the Greek word *proseuche*, which means oratory. We can sum this up in one word; speaking. Intercession in this same text is the Greek word *enteuxis,* which means an interview, or supplication. Intercession speaks of an interview with God on behalf of someone. An interview is a two-way form of communication. This means that you are in a conversation with the Holy Spirit and He is giving you back information, as opposed to just you speaking directly to God with no feedback. God has the "inside information" into that particular situation that you are interceding for and will 'download' it into your spirit through His Holy Spirit. You are reasoning together, as we saw Abraham doing in Genesis with God.

Now I will say again, intercession is made available to us all, but many do not move in it because of the great sacrifice that comes along with intercession. Interceding for someone or for a situation takes away from your own personal time and from your own issues. This takes putting aside all of your concerns about your own life and focusing on something or someone else. Again, many people are not willing to sacrifice their time for someone else.

For those who accept this call, you will move into another realm of intimacy with the Lord. God now sees your willingness and commitment to serve others instead of you first. This pleases God, so He will begin to prompt you through the Holy Spirit to intercede. It may be any time during the day or He could awaken you in the early morning hours to get up and intercede for someone. As you continue on, this will become a 'lifestyle' for you. You will get to a point where you just begin to intercede for a situation even if you have not heard from God to do so. This is where you enter into a place of spiritual maturity and move out!

Through all of this interaction between you and the Holy Spirit, people's lives and situations are being changed. Prayers are being answered, lives are being touched, families are being restored, suicides are being averted, and so much more. This angers satan and he will try any way that he possibly can to infiltrate your communion with God. As I said earlier, because you are hearing so much from God through His Spirit, pride can develop if you are not careful to guard yourself. You have to stay in the Word of God and in His face through prayer to know when He is speaking and when He is not.

You have the responsibility to seek God's face and find out if something that He has shared with you is to be released. If you move out prematurely and speak what God has not told you to, you can very well hinder, if not cause great harm to a situation. You have to be so in tuned with the Holy Spirit to operate in this fashion. We see from the prophet Jonah that God spoke clearly to him to go to Nineveh.

"Arise, go to Nineveh, that great city, and cry against it; for their wickedness has come up before Me." Jonah 1:2

Jonah decided not to heed the word of the Lord, but chose his own way.

"But Jonah arose to flee to Tarshish from the presence of the Lord. He went down to Joppa, and found a ship going to Tarshish; so he paid the fare, and went down into it, to go with them to Tarshish from the presence of the Lord." Jonah 1:3

We see in this scripture that God called the prophet Jonah to go and "speak" to the people of Nineveh, but he did everything in his natural power to get away from this responsibility. He wanted to get as far away as he could, so he paid money to catch a ship to Tarshish, which was the furthest city he could find on a ship from Nineveh. We find that no matter how far he tried to get away, He could not escape the Omnipresent God.

This story is in stark contrast to the story of Daniel. Daniel received dreams and visions from the Lord concerning different situations. God used him to interpret King Nebuchadnezzar's dreams, but he realized that the interpretation could only come from God, so he asked if they could give him some time to get the interpretation.

"So Daniel went in and asked the king to give him time, that he might tell the king the interpretation." Daniel 2:16

Now Daniel could have moved out in his flesh and made something up to escape death, but he knew that God was the only One who had the authority to interpret, so he went before the Lord for the answer. This is so very important, as we are hearing from God. The king's spirit bore witness to the interpretation, because it was true; from God, but if Daniel would have moved in haste, it could have cost him his life.

There is another instance in Daniel where the Lord sent him visions and they overwhelmed Daniel to the point of him falling on his face. In each of these visions, he was strengthened by angels and given instructions.

"Although I heard, I did not understand. Then I said, "My lord what shall be the end of these things?" v. 9-"And he said, "Go your way, Daniel, for the words are closed up and sealed till the time of the end." Daniel 1: 8-9

So we see from these two prophets that one was trying to run away from his responsibility to give God's Word in its proper season and the other moved in the spirit to such an extent of knowing when to speak and when not to speak. This is wisdom and God can use a yielded vessel, as Daniel was, to fulfill His plan in the earth.

As you begin to hear from the Spirit of God or see either through dreams or visions, allow God's wisdom to supersede all of the thoughts that can possibly enter into your mind. We have to guard our thoughts with all diligence because once satan knows that you are hearing from God to benefit someone else's life, he is going to try everything he knows to do to hinder that flow.

"casting down arguments and every high thing that exalts itself against the knowledge of God, bringing every thought into captivity to the obedience of Christ", v.6-"and being ready to punish all disobedience when your obedience is fulfilled." 2 Corinthians 10:5-6

This is the key; being obedient! God does not allow you this great insight into others' lives because you somehow earned it. No, God can only move in the earth realm through and obedient and submitted vessel, so instead of being puffed up because you know things that others may not, you need to abase yourself and remain broken before the Lord to continue hearing from Him.

I believe that my biggest downfall in the beginning was that I did not have anyone to teach me or to share with me their experiences concerning intercession or the prophetic. I was hearing and seeing so much, but I did not know how to walk this gift out effectively for the Lord. I kept hearing from so many people to be bold, but I was unsure of what that really meant. As time passed, I felt as if I was being disobedient because I had not released something and then, I would hear the word 'bold' again. So, instead of waiting on the Lord, I took this to mean that I needed to be "bold" and release it.

Needless to say, I did, but found out later that it was not the time, nor was it the correct word that I had released. This devastated me and I did not want to open my mouth anymore and did not want God to show me anything else again. Well, God was not moved by my immaturity or ignorance, so He continued to speak to me and He continued to show me things in my dreams. I thought that I had 'disqualified' myself, but what I failed to realize was that God knew ahead of time that I would miss the mark. What I failed to realize was that He called me before I was even conceived in my mother's womb. What I failed to realize, was that He is God and He can and will use whomever He chooses to use and that He chooses imperfect people to carry out His perfect will. Glory to God!

The reason that I am sharing all of this with you is because many people throughout history have given up on being used by God because they thought they had to be perfect. Well if we were perfect, then we would not need God. Do not get sidetracked because of your weaknesses or faults; we all have them. The awesome thing is to know that God uses us in spite of our nature. This is powerful!

"For you see your calling, brethren, that not many wise according to the flesh, not many mighty, not many noble are called," v.27-"But God has chosen the foolish things of the world to put to shame the wise, and God has chosen the weak things of the world to put to shame the things which are mighty." 1 Corinthians 1:26-27

So God chooses whom He pleases so that He will receive the glory and not man. He called you out, so that He could put His words in your mouth to give to a lost and dying world. We have to learn to get over ourselves and our insecurities and allow the Lord to use us however He chooses to use us. We saw when God called Moses that he was fearful and asked God, "Who am I that I should go to Pharaoh?" Exodus 3:11 He proceeded to ask God, "what shall I say to them?" Exodus 3:13 God then told Moses in verse 14a, "I AM THAT I

AM"....Thus shalt thou say unto the children of Israel, I AM hath sent me unto you."

This is why God speaks to you through these channels, so that you can lead them right back to Him. Anything that God tells you through His Spirit or in dreams or visions is to lead His people back to Him. If you are given the go ahead to release a word, you are to make sure that the person or people know that it is from God and God alone! You have to become disciplined in your walk with God to hear in this capacity; to know when and when not to speak. As I said in the previous chapters, this must come from spending time in His Word and in His presence on a consistent basis; it should be your lifestyle.

Another aspect that you should take into consideration is accountability. As I said earlier, I did not have anyone who shared with me how to move in this gift. What I learned was literally from trial and error, but I am here to let you know that when God calls you, He already has in place those who will cover the anointing on your life and pour into you all that you need to go forward. Not only that, but when He calls you, He calls you from a position of completeness. He has already perfected the gift in you before the foundations of the world. You will never have to think about what to say because if you are speaking for Him; His words will come out.

"But when they deliver you up, do not worry about how or what you should speak. For it will be given to you in that hour what you should speak;" v. 20-"for it is not you who speak, but the Spirit of your Father who speaks in you." Matthew 10:19-20

So if we would realize that there is no formula to proclaiming God's Word, that it is only by His Spirit, then we can rest our minds and stop thinking so much. Our only job is to obey what He has already told us to do, but we will know in our spirit if it is time to release or not. I wrestled one time with whether or not to reveal to someone what I had seen in a dream. Again, I kept hearing "be bold", but my spirit was unsettled. I thought that it was just because of what I saw, but the Spirit revealed to me that it was not time. If you have heard the Holy Spirit speak or you have seen a vision or a dream and your spirit is restless or you feel overwhelmed, it is NOT time to release it. You must get into the presence of the Lord and seek His wisdom for this particular situation. If you have not received peace in the matter, DO NOT MOVE!

Speaking to someone out of 'season' or time can greatly hinder the move of God in their life, as well as in your own. Connect yourself with someone in whom you are confident that the Spirit of the Lord abides in. Allow them to hold you accountable, but be open to be corrected if need be. If you trust the God enough in this individual to allow them to hold you accountable, then you should trust that God may very well speak correction through them into your life.

"So then, my beloved brethren, let every man be swift to hear, slow to speak, slow to wrath." James 1:19(emphasis mine)

Anyone who is not submitted to someone higher in spiritual discernment than himself is in reality a "rebel". You are considered a 'loose cannon' if you are not humble enough to receive from someone else, especially when God is speaking through them. No matter how 'high' you think you are operating in the spiritual realm, there is someone else in your life that has already been through what you are now experiencing. God has purposely placed them in your life as a "covering"; to mentor you in the gift that is in you.

Our man of God gave us an acronym a while ago that has taken root in my life; FAT. (Faithful, Available & Teachable) Now when God sees that you have been faithful in prayer and available to intercede; He will then send someone into your life to teach you, but you must be willing to hear. We must be willing to accept instruction, correction, and yes, even rebuke if the situation requires. Our whole purpose in this ministry is to merely be a "vessel" that God can freely move through with His Spirit. If we are not under authority and submission, He cannot and will not abide in us, but if you possess that faithful, available, and teachable spirit, He can and will move freely through you to speak to His people.

There are so many in the body of Christ who start out on fire for God and who submit themselves to His Spirit, but as soon as they begin to hear the word of the Lord, pride sets in and causes them to be totally removed from His presence. They think that they are moving mountains in the spiritual realm, but are in reality running a race on a treadmill; going nowhere. They are stagnant and ineffective because they have allowed the stench of pride to infiltrate their communion with the Holy Spirit. They have corrupted that direct line of incorruptible communication with the Father because of a spirit of pride. They think that they are the only ones who are hearing from God and have a word for everyone. Instead of spending time in the presence of the Lord seeking His wisdom on a situation, they immediately run out and share a word from the Lord. This is not only prideful, but this is outright arrogance and ignorance. Anyone who is not submitted to the leading of the Holy Spirit is not fit for the Kingdom of God, or the ministry of intercession.

I know that this may sound harsh to some, but it is absolutely necessary in the life of an intercessor. I am sharing this from a place of experience. I wanted so very much for God to use me. I wanted to hear from God and to do the work of the Kingdom, but I was spiritually immature when it came to hearing from Him and because of this, I acted on impulse at times, instead of being led by His Spirit. Yes, I was hearing from Him, but I was not covering it as I should and obtaining His wisdom for the word that He released to me. Why would God release a word to me knowing that I would miss it? In every ministry, you have to be tested. Through trial and error, experience is obtained. The real test is exposed when you find out who is willing to endure even after correction and rebuke is administered.

We see so many "wild bucks" in the body of Christ who after they have received correction, move out prematurely saying that the Lord told them to leave the ministry because the pastor or the bishop is holding them back. The devil is liar. Do not be deceived people. God is not going to tell you to leave a ministry because the man or woman of God that He set over you is holding you down. No! You must submit yourself not only to the leading of the Holy Spirit, but to the leading of the man or woman of God that has been assigned to your life. I found this out early on in the ministry. The woman that God placed over my life at that particular juncture saw right through me. She knew that I was immature in the things of God, and buckled me down in the presence of the Lord. I received correction and even though it felt terrible, I knew that it was God. Now even though I was immature when it came to intercession and hearing from God, I had enough foundation of the word in me to know that this was God correcting me through her.

I received the correction and began to move forward under the covering that God had placed over my life and I began to watch her. I began to imitate the things that I saw her do in intercession. Now many will say to you, "If it is really God operating through you, you will not have to imitate anyone." Now you can listen to the world or carnal Christian babble if you want to, but as for me, I obey the word and no one else. It is the Word of God that tells us specifically to imitate those of greater spiritual maturity.

"but imitate those who through faith and patience inherit the promises." Hebrews 6:12

As I submitted to her counsel, I did not take my eyes off of her. This woman of God operated powerfully in the realm of the Spirit. I knew that she reached heaven when she interceded. I saw her submit totally to the leading of the Holy Spirit and because of this, He placed boldness on her life, like none I had ever seen before. I desired to be bold like that in the Lord. Not that I wanted to be her, being that she is uniquely created by God and she can be replaced by no one, but the anointing that rested upon her life was powerful and my desire was to stay under her and learn from her. This is very important in the life of an intercessor. For you to know when and how to intercede effectively, you must be submitted to the guidance and wisdom of an experienced intercessor. You must humble yourself and attach yourself to someone whom God is moving powerfully through. Do not become jealous or even intimidated, but allow yourself to learn from them.

I was not privileged to stay under her tutelage for very long, but I held onto what I learned from her and moved on as the Holy

Spirit led our family. As we were led to our new ministry, I immediately connected with another awesome woman of God in whom the
Spirit of God dwelt. God will never leave you out there alone to carry
out His will in the earth. There are to be no lone rangers in the body of
Christ; this is out of order. As I watched this woman of God enter into
intercession; everything on the inside of me began to shift. That
boldness that I asked God for previously was beginning to take root. I
was intimidated at first because I had never seen such power operating
in intercession, but I humbled myself and connected myself to her
guidance and began to seek her wisdom in the ministry of intercession.

Why I am sharing all of this with you? Because again, if you
are not submitted to someone of greater spiritual authority, you will
not know the boundaries of your influence and you can very well self-
destruct. As I said before, accountability is an important aspect of the
intercessory ministry. When you are able to connect to someone in
whom you can trust, they will impart their wisdom into your life and
give you greater insight into a situation and help you cover it. This is
not a game and this is not a contest of who is hearing from the Lord
greater. The devil is a liar! This is a very weighty assignment and you
do not want to be held accountable to God for not completing it or
even worse, for doing it your own way and causing harm to a situation
or individual.

*"It would be better for him if a millstone were hung around his
neck, and he were thrown into the sea, than that he should offend one
of these little ones." Luke 17:2*

The lives of the people in whom God will have you to intercede for are precious to Him. There will be times when He will ask
you to cover new converts to guard and to protect them from the taunts
and tricks of the enemy. They are babies in this walk, so they may not
necessarily know when satan is on attack. It is your job to stand in the
gap for them and to cover them until they pass through that temptation.
Now in the midst of this, being that this is a babe in Christ, instead of
releasing to them the avenue in which satan will attack, you are to
encourage them with the word of God for that situation and allow them
to grow. If you prematurely release to them the pathway in which the

enemy will come, it could very cause them to stumble. Just as the above scripture stated, "It would better for you if a millstone were hung around your neck." We have to count the costs of our ministry. Are we willing to do all that it takes to complete the assignment that God has given to us?

Now as you begin to accept the call of intercession, obey the leading of the Holy Spirit, and allow your own agendas to be diverted for the glory of God, He will open up areas of intercession on greater levels. The people and the situations that He will have you to cover may become more of burden to you if you allow yourself to get in the way. The Lord began to speak to me concerning someone who was very close to me, but someone who was in a great level of authority. When I heard the Lord say to me what the situation was, I became infuriated in the spirit. I was livid that the enemy had the nerve to attack this person in this area. I began immediately to enter into intercession on behalf of this individual. Because I allowed myself to be moved emotionally by the situation, I allowed the main one who I was rebuking to enter in. Instead of allowing the Holy Spirit to grant me wisdom and insight into the matter, I moved out in ignorance and released the word. I am not ashamed to reveal this to you because just as Jesus said in scripture, "For this cause was I sent", I understand that I went through all of this, because God knew that I would be here today, writing this book. Glory to God!

Now being that this individual was spiritually mature, they were not moved by the revelation of my mistake, but this did not excuse me from being corrected by the Lord. To be chastised by the Lord is a good thing. Many will have a hard time accepting that chastisement is a good thing for you. It may not feel good, but I can guarantee you that it will benefit you in the long run. We can look to our children and see that correcting them now will lead them to make the right decisions later in life. They may not understand it now, but when they are on their own, they will remember what you told them and they will, in turn, apply it to their lives. They may not think that you love them at the moment, but God will reveal it to them in due time. So it is with God. Correction is necessary and will only help you out in the ministry of intercession.

"For whom the LORD loves He chastens, And scourges every son whom He receives." Hebrews 12:6

We see here that it says that He only chastens and scourges His sons. We think that God should be busy out there correcting the sinners and blessing us because we are His sons, but it is quite the contrary. God gives us free will and He is not going to correct you if you do not make the decision to lay down your life and follow Him. He only corrects those who make the decision to give their lives over to Him and trust Him that He knows what is best for us now that we are His sons. Trust Him, trust the Holy Spirit, and trust those in whom God has placed over your life to cover you. If you desire to be used by the Lord to build the Kingdom of God in this earth and your sole purpose in hearing from Him is to benefit the Kingdom of God, humble yourself, submit, and receive correction if necessary, and you will bring glory to His name. You have been entrusted with a great assignment. Will you answer the call?

HOLINESS:

'BE YE HOLY...FOR I AM HOLY'

"because it is written, 'Be holy, for I am holy."
1Peter 1:16

"To me the greatest privilege in all the world would be perfect holiness. If I had my choice of all the blessings I can conceive of, I would choose perfect conformity to the Lord Jesus, or, in one word, holiness." – Charles Spurgeon

Once we understand that we are to be disciplined, held accountable, and under authority, then we are able to move on to a deeper level of intimacy with the Father. The Word of God in 1Peter 1:16 says, "Be holy, for I am holy." Holiness is not something that we are born with. We all came into this world and immediately took on the sinful nature of this world. The Word of God says, "Be Holy", which is not a suggestion, but a command. The command here is coming from a Holy God to an unholy people. We see that he called us in an unholy state; fully aware of all of our weaknesses and faults. Why would God call us to an assignment knowing full well that we may eventually miss the mark?

I am glad that you asked. God will not share His glory with anyone. He speaks to imperfect people to get His perfect message into the earth realm. Just as we saw from the beginning, God needs a man in the earth to just 'accept' the call, regardless of his shortcomings. As He continues to speak to this submitted 'vessel', he or she will learn how to speak and conduct themselves in a holy manner. Because of the intimate communion with the Lord, we become fully aware that the message that we are speaking is not our own, but the Lord's, so we return the glory back to Him.

We also saw from this scripture that it says, "in all manner of conversation." So we see here that no part of our conversation is off limits to God's correction. We are to be transforming the way that we speak everyday; it is a process. Now this does not mean that you can take your time changing or just change what you feel needs to change. If we are meditating on the Word of God on a consistent basis and fellowshipping on a regular basis with the Lord in prayer, then our conversation will reflect it. There is a saying that says, "You are what you eat". Whatever it is that is occupying the majority of your time, is what you will become. If you are watching four and five hours of television a day and only giving God five or ten minutes, what do you think is going to come out of you?

We cannot complain and say that this lifestyle of following Christ is not working if we are not investing the necessary time into cultivating it. We can go to a movie and sit for two to three hours in the dark and not fall asleep, but sit down for five minutes to read the Word of God with every light in the house on and fall right to sleep with our Bible right on top of us. How can this be? I am glad that you asked.

Holiness, in its simplest meaning, can be expressed as self-control under the leading of the Holy Spirit. Charles Haddon Spurgeon, an eighteenth century preacher says it this way:

A man gets a degree of holiness -- holiness of outward conduct in regeneration. He henceforth does not lie, or swear, 'or steal, or get drunk, or willfully sin in regeneration. But real holiness goes deeper than the outer conduct, and cleanses us from the indwelling sin. That inbred sin principle which fights against our piety and makes us jealous, and revengeful, and willful, and passionate, and hot-tempered, and selfish, and self-indulgent, must be and is consumed by the fire of the Holy Ghost before we have the holiness described in the text that makes us "holy like God," and "pure as He (Christ) is pure." -- It is a Possible Holiness.[3]

This type of lifestyle comes with a price tag. You are going to have to discipline yourself and make great sacrifices if you desire to hear from the Lord in order to impact this earth. This is why I believe that God sent His Son because He saw that no one else was willing to discipline themselves or sacrifice their time to intercede for the people and situations of the earth.

"He saw that there was no man, And wondered that there was no intercessor; Therefore His own arm brought salvation for Him; And His own righteousness, it sustained Him." Isaiah 59:16

We see that it says, "He wondered that there was no intercessor." This implies that He was speaking to the people, but why were they not interceding? Why would they not 'accept' the call? Why, because they were not willing to sacrifice their own time to change the world around them. They lacked discipline and self-control because they were only concerned with their needs, wants, and desires being fulfilled. So God, in His holiness, sent forth His Holy Son Jesus, who was the embodiment of Himself.

We are by nature a selfish people. We want so much from God, but we are unwilling to give Him just a few hours a day in prayer or a portion of our sleep to intercede for someone else. Many of us "Christians" give the bare minimum, so that we can check it off on our list that we have done it. We are missing the whole point of communing with our heavenly Father through His Holy Spirit.

We see from Matthew Chapter 26 where Jesus asked His disciples to set up to watch and pray, but they did not possess the discipline or self-control needed to do so.

"Then He came to the disciples and found them sleeping, and said to Peter, "What! Could you not watch with Me one hour?" v.41- "Watch and pray, lest you enter into temptation. The spirit is indeed willing, but the flesh is weak." Matthew 26:40-41

Jesus was upset with the disciples because they lacked the self-control to watch just one hour with Him. It goes on to say in verses 42-45 that He had to go back three times to pray without the support of His disciples. Each time that He woke them up to pray; He would find them again sleeping. This is what we are still doing to God to this day. He is still calling on us to pray and to intercede, but our lack of self-control and discipline is causing us to miss our 'appointments' with the Holy Spirit. How many of your prayers are going unanswered because you refuse to spend quality time in His presence? How many precious lives are lost because you refused to get up and intercede when God called you out of your sleep?

This is serious. We cannot blow these situations off and say that "it must have been God's will" or that "I guess God cannot use me". God's desire is for NO man to be lost and for no man to die in his sin. He explains all throughout the Word of God that His desire for us is to prosper and to live. Again, it is merely a lack of self-control, but we can also take this a little further and classify it as denial. Many of us know that God is speaking to us, but we refuse to accept it by saying, "He can't be speaking to me?" We need to quickly get over ourselves and realize that God calls us according to the way He created us, not from the way we currently see ourselves.

"For I know the thoughts that I think toward you, saith the Lord, thoughts of peace, and not of evil, to give you an expected end." Jeremiah 29:11, KJV

So God's thoughts of us are not our thoughts of ourselves. His expected end for you is Holiness, which by the way was also His beginning for you. Glory to God! The Word of God says that "I am the Alpha and the Omega, the Beginning and the End." Revelation 1:8a If we would just trust in the Word of God and take it as it is, we would understand that in Genesis it says, "Then God said, Let Us make man in Our image, according to Our likeness…" Genesis 1:26

If He is the Beginning and the End and you were created in His image and in His likeness, then when He said, "Be holy for I am holy", you are to be just that; Holy! Why? You were made to be just like Him.

Holiness can take on many different forms. We will cover just a few of them here. The first one that we will discuss is the gateway of the mouth. We touched a little on this previously in the aspect of our conversation, but let us look at it from another perspective. What we physically put into our mouths can also hinder us from hearing clearly from the Lord. So much of what we eat today is processed and full of chemicals. We have to eat healthy in order to be healthy; mind, body, and soul. Fresh fruits and vegetables give us the needed nutrients that allow us to see, hear, and live better. There are many anointed men and women of God that are being raised in this hour to "teach" us Godly eating habits because we are missing this aspect of our Christian walk. We are doing everything "right" according to our standards, but we are dying prematurely because we are refusing the wisdom of God in this particular area.

"I beseech you therefore, brethren, by the mercies of God, that you present your bodies a living sacrifice, holy, acceptable to God, which is your reasonable service." Romans 12:1

Have you ever gone out to eat at a fast-food restaurant and found that you were extremely tired after eating? This is most evident if you have not eaten like this in a while. Your body does not recognize this "foreign" food and either it will cause your stomach to hurt, or make you extremely sleepy. Our minds process clearly depending on many issues, but one of them is how we eat. Our minds should be clear and focused at all times in order to hear clearly from the Holy Spirit. The Word says, 'present your bodies as a living sacrifice', which implies that there is something greater that you are seeking by doing so.

The next area that we will deal with is the gateway of the mouth and our conversation. There is so much power in our words. We do not realize the impact of our words and how they form our very lives. We saw from 1 Peter 1:16 that the Word says "be holy in ALL manner of conversation. (Emphasis mine) So, we must choose carefully the words that we speak. Yes we are called in our 'imperfect' state, but we are not called to stay in this state forever, but to grow and mature in holiness. The words that we speak should produce life and not death.

"Death and life are in the power of the tongue, And those who love it will eat its fruit." Proverbs 18:21

For holiness to be evident in our lives, we must be speaking life and not death. This means speaking positive, faith-filled words, instead of negative words that are filled with unbelief. Holiness can only become a part of you if you are speaking or confessing godly words over your life on a consistent basis. It has to become you; the more you say it, the more you are going to believe it and walk in it. Again, we saw how our mouths have the power to frame our world. We just have to be trained and keep it always before us and not just say it, but LIVE it!

"For with the heart one believes unto righteousness, and with the mouth confession is made unto salvation." Romans 10:10

This scripture says with your heart you believe that you are in right standing with God, but it takes you opening up your mouth and confessing it to be saved. The same principle applies to walking in holiness; believe with your heart and confess with your mouth.

Now we will study the gateway of the eye. As we touched upon earlier, "You are what you eat"; whatever you spend the most of your time watching or doing, this will frame your thoughts and actions. There are so many avenues that the enemy has crept into these days, including television, movies, and the internet.

The gateway of the eye is a very dangerous entryway, if we do not guard it with all diligence. The images that are scanned through our eyesight are immediately sent to our brains where they are processed and downloaded. Now it becomes a part of our thought process and a permanent fixture in our imagination. We start early on with our children, guarding what they watch on television because we do not want them exposed to anything that will harm them. This process should never end because we become older. There is no age that is appropriate to view harmful things. The world has established a ratings system when it comes to movies and television, but our ratings system is the incorruptible Word of God! Glory to God! There are three main entryways that satan uses to tempt us in and we need to be aware of them and able to discern when we are being targeted.

"For all that is in the world-the lust of the flesh, the lust of the eyes, and the pride of life-is not of the Father but is of the world."
1 John 2:16

The Word says that these three things are all that is in this world and we see from them the "gateways" that they enter in through. How can we walk in holiness if we are watching any and every thing? None of us are exempt from temptation, so we have to consistently guard ourselves on a daily basis. We have to know what we can and cannot watch. We have to know that holiness is a lifestyle, so there have to be boundaries set that we refuse to cross over. The gateway of the eye is a major entryway that the enemy tempts men in; not all, but many.

The enemy understands that if he can get them "trapped" in pornography and such; that they will not walk in the holiness that God desires for them. These are not just non-believers, but these are men who have given their lives over to God, but who are struggling with unconfessed sin in their lives. Women can and do deal with this same issue, but satan will usually try to get us in other areas. The underlying issue is that again, "We are what we eat (see)".

The last gateway that we will discuss is the gateway of the ear. We hear so many things throughout our day. With the eyes, we have a greater control over what we see because we can merely turn off what we are watching or turn away from something that we know we should not see, but hearing is a totally different entryway into our lives. There are many times throughout our day where we hear gossip, backbiting, cursing, and every foul thing that can possibly come out of someone's mouth, but we cannot turn it off. Whether we are at work, school, or just out in the community, we cannot control someone else's conversation. This is where we have to be guarded with the Word of God and allow it to cover us when we are encountered with these situations.

"So then faith comes by hearing, and hearing by the word of God." Romans 10:17

It says that faith comes by hearing, but it goes on to say and hearing by the Word of God. So we see here that faith does not come by hearing just anything, but by hearing the Word of God. It also implies that you cannot just hear one time and get what you need to get. It has to be on a consistent basis that you are hearing what God needs for you to hear. If you are in a situation where what you are hearing is not godly or just not something that you should be hearing altogether, the Word that you have in you should counteract or overshadow what it is that you have just heard. You do not have to be drawn into it because you have been covered already through your intimate time spent in the Word of God and in His presence through prayer.

Another area that we need to cover when it comes to the gateway of the ear is the company that we keep. We have to guard ourselves continually. We should not be spending the majority of our time with non-believers or even with Christians who are not on the level that you are on. I don't say this to mean that you are better than anyone because you are not, but what I am saying is spend quality time with those in whom you know to share your experiences as an intercessor or with those in whom you know will cover you and pour into you; not those who will tear you down and bring you down into their situations. There has to be accountability, as we discussed earlier. Your faith in what God is doing in and through you will not come by spending time with people who are not speaking faith-filled words of encouragement into your life.

All of these gateways are vitally important when it comes to walking in Holiness. We have to ensure that we are covering every area that the enemy can enter into, so that he cannot move us out of the place of authority that comes with living a holy lifestyle.

As an intercessor you will encounter many who are in opposition to your ministry, including many within the church itself. As I said earlier, we are all called to intercede, but many do not accept the call because it requires a great deal of sacrifice and self-denial. You will find at times people in the church looking at you like you are crazy because of your passion in intercessory ministry, mostly through the gift of your heavenly language. It is available to us all, but again, many do not receive the manifestation because of unbelief or just because they are afraid of it. You should not be moved by this, but continue allowing your lifestyle to display the character of holiness in all that you say and do.

I hear so many people outside of the church and even some in the house of God who say that you are acting "holier than thou". Well let me share something with you; this is the heart of God Himself. Now this does not mean that you act as if you are God Himself or that you are better than anyone else, but what it does mean is that we are to hold a standard up to the world showing them that we are His Sons. There are many times throughout scripture where it shows how passionate Jesus was about us displaying holiness. It shows in John 17:17 that Jesus prayed for it-"Sanctify them by Your truth. Your word is truth." Sanctify means to be set apart for His use; purify or holy. In Matthew 5:48, Jesus commanded it-"Therefore you shall be perfect, just as your Father in heaven is perfect." Perfect in this verse means completeness as defined in mental and moral character; holy. In 1 Thessalonians 4:7, He calls us to it-"For God did not call us to uncleanness, but in holiness." The reference here is defined as sanctification, purification, and holiness. He then promises it in 1 Thessalonians 5:23a-24b-"Now may the God of peace Himself sanctify you completely........who will also do it." Sanctify in this verse means hallow or be holy. He lastly died for it-"and declared to be the Son of God with power according to the spirit of holiness, by the resurrection from the dead." Romans 1:4 Holiness in this verse is also described as sacred, which is also translated as holy.

This reveals to us the major importance of holiness in the life of the Believer, but more importantly in the life of an intercessor. We have to have our hands 'clean' and our lives 'spotless'. Does this mean that we will never make mistakes? No. But what it does mean is that our "name" should be held in great respect amongst the non-believers, as well as in the house of the Lord. When God begins to reveal things to you for you to release, how will people receive you? Will your name hold the weight of the assignment that is given you? Now some will not receive the word no matter what your character, but you are still required to uphold that standard for the glory of God; you are His Son.

Another area that the enemy tries to attack intercessors in is through pride. As you continue dwelling in the presence of God and His Spirit on a consistent basis, you are going to "hear", as well as "see" many things about different people and situations. God will begin to reveal through His Spirit in great detail the things that He desires for you to intercede for, but you must not allow this to become a stumbling block in your life. You are not hearing and seeing in this manner because you have been so good or that you deserve in some way to receive it. It is only because you are submitted and obedient to His Spirit. Does He still desire for you to progress into holiness? Yes, but this is not the prerequisite for Him calling you as an intercessor. As I said earlier, He calls us in an imperfect state, so that His perfect will can be established in our lives.

Another example of being holy is to separate yourself according to the choice you made to follow the Lord. Not only are you to guard the gateways of your eyes, ears, and mouth, as well as remove things and people in your life that will hinder you, but you must also separate yourself unto the Lord in service. The assignment must be more important to you than anything or anyone, and pleasing the Lord should be the foremost priority in your life. Living a life of holiness sets you apart and causes the Spirit of God to rest mightily upon your life, allowing the Lord to use you to impact an unholy world. We see in Numbers 6:5, how the word of God describes the Nazarite.

"All the days of the vow of his separation no razor shall come upon his head; until the days are fulfilled for which he separated himself to the LORD, he shall be holy. Then he shall let the locks of the hair of his head grow."

A Nazarene lifestyle is defined as an institution that was a symbol of a life devoted to God and separated from all sin; a holy life. We look in the word and have been taught for so long that this is a lifestyle that was only for a select few in the Old Testament days, but the Greek word for Nazarite is *nazoraios*, which has only one meaning; Christian. So if we consider ourselves Christian, then we should consider ourselves as Nazarites; living a life devoted to God and separate from all sin; holy. When you begin to set yourself apart as holy and separate yourself unto the Lord, He will begin to separate you into the calling that He has purposed over your life.

In the series entitled, "Separate Yourself: Be Holy"[4], Dr. Kristie A. Moreland elaborated in depth on the necessity of holiness in the life of a believer. She stated,

"If we are to go to greater levels of intimacy with the Father, then we are going to have to separate ourselves from the distractions of this world and separate ourselves unto the Lord."

She stated how pertinent it is to remove ourselves from fellowship that will hinder us from obtaining the promises of God. She went on further to discuss that it is not only those on the outside of the church that we need to separate ourselves from, but also some of those in the Body of Christ.

We have to understand that not everyone in the Body of Christ is mature in the things of God. Not all that enter into those doors on

Sunday morning or for midweek service are coming for the same reasons that you are coming. You have to value what God is imparting into your life to the extent of yes, even separating yourself within the four walls of the church. Does this mean that you ignore people, act as if you are better than someone else, or even look down upon them; absolutely not! But what it does mean is that you need to know who you can share your thoughts and concerns with and who you cannot. You need to be able to guard yourself against any outside influence that satan may be sending to distract you from the assignment that the Lord has you on. As I stated earlier, this comes from a lifestyle of discipline.

Separate means to remove or sever from association or service. There are two Hebrew words that I want us to look at. The first is the word *badal*, which means to divide, separate, distinguish, or differ. The second being *nazar*, which is the root of Nazarite, meaning to hold aloof, abstain, to set apart, devote, or consecrate. As an intercessor, you are to abstain from things that are not pleasing to the Lord. You should have a lifestyle where others can look at you and distinguish you as a person who is devoted to God. You are no longer living an ordinary life of a Christian, but you have now entered into another dimension in Christ and because of you setting yourself apart from the foolish things of this world, God will begin to set you apart for His glory. This is the point where He begins to put His words in your mouth and where He begins to release a greater level of anointing upon your life. He will begin to put you on display; not for your benefit or recognition, but for His glory and for His purpose.

We saw from the life of Samuel how he was set apart for the Lord at a very early age. We know the story of Hannah, how she prayed and asked the Lord to give her a male child. She was unable to have any children and she wept almost daily because her soul desire was to have a child. Hannah went to the temple to pray unto God on behalf of her childless womb, but she went on further to declare to God that if He granted her the desire of her heart, that she would offer her only son back to the Lord for the rest of his life.

"Then she made a vow and said, "O LORD of hosts, if You will indeed look on the affliction of Your maidservant and remember me, and not forget Your maidservant, but will give Your maidservant a male child, then I will give him to the LORD all the days of his life, and no razor shall come upon his head." 1 Samuel 1:11

Hannah chose to separate her unborn child to the Lord. She vowed to God that Samuel would serve Him all the days of his life. She devoted her son to the Lord and he ministered before the priest, Eli. Samuel grew daily in the Lord and the scripture says that "he was in favour both with the Lord, and also with men." (1 Samuel 2:26) It goes on to say that Eli the priest had two sons, Hophni and Phinehas. His sons did not know the Lord and they did evil things unto the people of Israel. Eli did confront his sons and asked them not to do these things, but they did not listen. Eli had a choice at this point to banish his sons from the temple, but he chose not to do so; therefore, the Lord sent a messenger to him to warn him of what was about to happen to his sons.

We see here that there can be those even in the house of the Lord who are not devoted or who have not separated themselves apart for the Lord, but who come for their own selfish motives and gain. Now it does not mention it in the Bible, but we must assume that because Samuel was being reared by the priest Eli that he had to have come in contact with his sons at some point. Was he influenced by Hophni and Phinehas? Did Samuel allow their behavior to change the way he ministered before their father or even to the Lord? Well we see from the word of God that Samuel continued to grow day by day in the things of God and that he was even used by God to prophesy to Eli of his sons impending death, so no matter what it was that the brothers did, Samuel remained faithful to his call and to the Lord.

As an intercessor, you will be challenged to follow the crowd. As I said earlier, many will be offended by the call on your life and many even to the point of dislike or hate. When you set yourself apart as holy unto the Lord and begin to only concern yourself with pleasing the Lord and fulfilling His purpose over your life, you must be ready for opposition. Samuel heard a word from the Lord and at first was concerned about sharing with Eli what the Lord had said unto him, but he remained obedient. I have found myself more times than I can count battling with being who I am in front of others, not outside of the church, but actually in the house of the Lord. When I came back to the Lord after years of rebelling against the Lord, I made a commitment to serve Him wholeheartedly. The time that I spent with Him grew greater and greater by the day and my love for Him abounded. I began to pray more, study more, and worship Him like I had never worshipped Him before. I noticed as I attended services that people would look at me very strange. Whether it was praise or worship going on, I saw myself to be one of very few that were submitted to this time with the Lord. As an intercessor or just a believer in general, you should be sold out to this precious time with God, but the sad reality is that many are not. If we say that we love the Lord and are serving the Lord, we should look like we mean it. Now there are still some who look as if they are submitted in worship, but are far from the Lord in their heart, but this is not our concern. What I am trying to convey to you is that no matter what anyone else is doing, you are to stay true to who you are. Do not be ashamed of what God has placed on the inside of you. If He is in you, then He should be coming out of you. Glory to God!

Once I began to mature in things of God, I was given a greater responsibility within the house of God. My eyes were opened before to many things that were going on in the church, but the level of discernment shifted greatly after this point. Now that I could see the faces of the people directly, I was seeing a greater level of resentment and opposition to my relationship with Christ. Before I was raised up in leadership, I was faithful and obedient to my relationship with God and I moved in intercession without the prompting of anyone, but the Holy Spirit Himself. I noticed how others would stare at me and they probably thought that I was crazy. I am sure that many of you intercessors have experienced the same things in your own church. I did not allow this to distract me or to move me out of the position that God had me in at that time and that was standing in the gap. As I became a leader within the church, I saw this adversity go to another level. Even the leaders within the house found me strange, if you will. You may hear some tell you, "It does not take all of that" or "Please, it is not that serious". Well to them it may very well not take all of that and it may not be serious to them, but I am here to tell you to be bold and to set yourself apart from those who do not stand with you in the assignment that God has placed on your life. I am absolutely not telling you to be arrogant or prideful because this is not of God, but stand firm in who you are and in what He has called you to do and be a constant example of Christ in their lives.

You must set yourself apart as holy, so that God can use you for His glory. You must set yourself apart as holy, so that others will see an example of Christ to become. You must set yourself apart as holy, so that God's plans and purposes will be made manifest in the earth realm through you. Again, God cannot operate in the earth realm without a submitted, committed, obedient, and yes, holy vessel. He is a holy God and He will not move through an unholy vessel. Now we all are imperfect and no one of us is without sin, but we must be maturing and changing daily to become holy as He is. As you avail yourself to Him in consecrating yourself, He will release a covering over your life that allows you to discipline yourself. God will not do it all for us, but what He will do is meet us as we have stepped out in obedience to His word. Once you separate yourself unto Him; He will separate you for the assignment over your life.

"And you shall be holy to Me, for I the LORD am holy, and have separated you from the peoples, that you should be Mine."
Leviticus 20:26

You will begin to see, as you make the choice to separate yourself from others in and out of the body of Christ that God will begin to further separate you in every area of your life. You have to make the choice of what is more important to you; God or man. You have to be willing to sacrifice your friends, your family, and even those who are supposed to be your brothers and sisters in Christ, to fulfill God's ultimate plan for your life and for the Kingdom of God to be established in the earth. You must be willing to lay down your life; your needs, wants, and desires, to stand in the gap for the people of this earth, the body of Christ, and the lost souls of this world.

All God is looking for is someone who will set themselves apart and allow Him to move through them. There is nothing that He will withhold from you as you submit to becoming holy in His sight. You must see your sacrifice and obedience as a means to bringing others into the knowledge of His holiness. You must see yourself as a tool that God is using to teach His people. This does not come cheap; there is a price to pay in order for God's purposes to be established in the earth. Look to your big brother Jesus and you will see the price that He chose to pay, so that you could enter into eternal glory with Him. You must see the assignment that God has called you to not only as important, but necessary for your destiny fulfillment and the fulfillment of His Kingdom in the earth. Do not take it lightly.

"Is it a small thing to you that the God of Israel has separated you from the congregation of Israel, to bring you near to Himself, to do the work of the tabernacle of the LORD, and to stand before the congregation to serve them;" Numbers 16:9

You have been called to serve not only God, but to serve the body of Christ through intercession. God says to us, "Is this not important enough to set yourself apart as holy", so that you can draw closer to Him, to work in the house of the Lord, and to serve the body of Christ? You must make a choice and decide if you are willing to accept the call of intercession and once you do; you must know that setting yourself apart unto holiness is necessary for the call. You must make up in your mind that no matter what others may think of you; you are on assignment. You must lay aside your feelings and emotions and allow the Spirit of God to lead you and guide you in everything that you say and do. You must be determined to do what the Spirit tells you to do, no matter what area of your life that it pertains to.

We can look to the life of Joseph, the youngest son of Jacob, as one who was separated for the work of the Lord. Joseph was his father's favorite son. At a young age, his father made him a coat of many colors that signified his favor over his son Joseph, and his brothers hated him because of this. Joseph began to have dreams concerning the future state, not only of his family, but of the call of God on his life. He shared with his family what the dreams were and they were very angry with him because of this. It came to a point of them conspiring to kill Joseph because of their jealousy and envy of him. We see the entire process unfold in Genesis from Chapter thirty seven all the way through Genesis Chapter fifty. We see how the transpiring of events in Joseph's journey; from him being thrown into the pit, sold to the Ishmaelites, sold into Potiphar's house, being imprisoned, and finally brought before Pharaoh to interpret his dreams, were a holy set up from God Himself.

God separated Joseph before he was even conceived in his mother's womb. He had a plan for Joseph's life and even though we look at how Joseph came to become a ruler in Pharaoh's house as extreme, it was all necessary to not only confirm His word through Joseph, but to humble his family and allow them to see the God that reigned over Joseph's life. How many of us are willing to set ourselves apart to the extent that Joseph did? How many of us are willing to be talked about, hated, and even persecuted for living a life of holiness? How many of us are willing to sacrifice our lives now, so that we can enter into the promise as Joseph did? God has a plan for your life and that plan is connected to many other people. Joseph could have only thought of himself and complained to the Lord about what he had to go through, but Joseph understood the weight of his assignment and that it was bigger than him.

"But when it pleased God, who separated me from my mother's womb and called me through His grace," Galatians 1:15

God called Joseph to be different. He desired others to see him set apart, so that they could see a distinction between the holy and the unholy. God cannot be in the earth, so He needs an example of Himself in the earth that others can imitate; therefore, drawing unto Him. You have a great responsibility as an intercessor to set yourself apart as holy. Many may be watching you and many may very well talk about you, but you must know what God has said to you, as Joseph did. I am sure that his brothers called him everything but a child of God, but he did not allow this to distract him or move him out of his position. He was on assignment for the Lord and he endured all of the trials, temptations, and persecutions that were sent His way. Because he obeyed the voice of the Lord, God divinely protected Joseph all the way to Pharaoh's house. Through all of the accusations of unholy people, Joseph stood firm and trusted in the Lord. He did not back down or give in to what others would say.

Hilary Amara, in her book "What Will People Say"[5], hit the target concerning a life that is set apart. She graciously reveals to the reader that you cannot be concerned with what is going on in the "Marketplace"; what others are saying, but to stay focused on the mission that God has you on.

If you get caught up with what others are saying, you will be intimidated and forget about your great testimonies and history with God.

She goes on to say:

So many people compromise in many areas of their lives just because they are concerned about what people will say. We should not do things just because we want to impress or please others. There are a lot of ways that we fall into this trap and we can never be able to please God if we are so concerned about what people will say.

Again, God has called you to be obedient and to please Him, not others. Your life must be hidden with Christ (Colossians 3:3) and your priority should be that of fulfilling the assignment that God has graced you with. You cannot be concerned with what others say to you or even about you. You truly become to know Whose you are when others are coming up against you. If you do not have adversity knocking at your back door, then you need to ask yourself if you are walking in the will of God for your life. If you are fulfilling the call of God on your life, persecutions must come, so that God's glory can be released into your life.

"Yes, and all who desire to live godly in Christ Jesus will suffer persecution." 2 Timothy 3:12

It says that all those who desire to live godly. We saw from the beginning of this chapter that the word says, "Be ye holy, for I am holy". To live a godly life is to live like God and to do so, we must set ourselves apart from this evil world and take on the nature of Him, and that is a holy one. Allow the Lord to use you for His glory and avail yourself to the leading of His Holy Spirit through it all. For you to become holy, you must know how to be holy. You are not born holy; you have to become holy and that can only be obtained through reading the Word of God and being transformed daily through the power of that word. You also must be renewed through receiving the Gift of the Holy Spirit, which is your utmost example in being able to discern between right and wrong; He leads you and guides you as you hear from Him. You are not alone. He says that He will never leave you nor forsake you. (Hebrews 13:5)

Guard yourself in all that you do and make discipline one of your highest priorities as an intercessor. God will guard you, as you guard yourself. The goal is to mature daily in the things of God where you are able to move effectively in His will and to be that light to a dying world. As they see you becoming holy unto God, they too will follow in your example. Do not become impatient or discouraged. As you submit yourself to His will of being holy, He will do His part. He is faithful and just and He is for you. Know that in all that you do, God is with you.

> *"Therefore 'Come out from among them, And be separate, says the Lord. Do not touch what is unclean, And I will receive you."*2 Corinthians 6:17

He gives us a command and in return He tells us what He will do for us. We must go through the process of becoming holy if we desire to fulfill the call of intercession on our lives. For you to be effective in the earth realm on behalf of others and situations, you must go to a greater dimension in your own personal walk with the Lord and pursue a lifestyle of holiness. You must be holy in the way you think, talk, walk, dress, eat, give, and love. God will never ask you to become holy in one area and leave out the rest because they all exist in harmony with the heart of God; if one area is left out, then it is not holy. Continue daily being transformed because it is a process, but know that as you step out in obedience, God is standing on the other side waiting to help you across. Do not give up, but press your way towards that great promise over your life. You are a son of God and He desires to use you mightily in the earth.

> *"and that you put on the new man which was created according to God, in true righteousness and holiness." Ephesians 4:24*

As you submit yourself to His will for your life and choose the road of holiness, God will open many doors to you and He will use you greatly in the earth realm to bring His Kingdom to pass here; as it is in Heaven. Will you answer the call?

✂PRAYER AND FASTING✂

"and this woman was a widow of about eighty-four years, who did not depart from the temple, but served God with fastings and prayers night and day."

Luke 2:37

The scripture above speaks of Anna, a prophetess from the tribe of Asher, who was of great age, a faithful widower, and one who regularly ministered in the house of the Lord. As we saw from the last Chapter, holiness is the most important characteristic of an intercessor. Anna the prophetess could very well be classified as one of the first great intercessors in the life of Jesus. She came boldly confessing Him before the people in the temple, so we must assume that she had received "insight" from God concerning Him. The scripture says that she "served God with fastings and prayers night and day." One who spends this much time in the presence of the Lord is going to hear greatly from the Spirit of God. Insight and Revelation will come to you as you are obedient to meet with the Father daily.

No matter how you think your prayer life is, whether it is "seasoned" or not, is not the issue. What is important to God is your willingness and obedience to pray and intercede when He calls you. We have all grown up and heard our mothers, grandmothers, and others in the church declare 'great' and 'powerful' prayers that we thought we could never imitate. We always felt as if we could not pray better than someone else or even come close, so we just refused to pray. This is not what God is concerned with because no matter how good someone sounds, it does not mean that their heart is in tune with the heart of God.

From the last Chapter on Holiness, we saw how the enemy uses the three gateways; the mouth, the eyes, and the ears (lust of the flesh, lust of the eyes, and the pride of life) to try and distract us from receiving instructions from the Holy Spirit in intercession. In these last days, we are seeing a great move of the enemy to 'satisfy' our senses, so as to move us out of a position of holiness. Prayer and fasting has to be a part of the intercessor's lifestyle. We saw earlier how prayer is defined as a direct communication between you and the Father. This is time where you fellowship intimately with Him and gain awareness of who you are in Him. This time represents the relationship between Father and child and gives a connotation of having "history" with God.

This is so very crucial because as an intercessor, you are reasoning with the Lord on behalf of peoples and situations. If you have no "history" with the Father, how can He trust you with the true riches of His Kingdom? Abraham interceded for Sodom and because he was in covenant with God; God remembered his prayer and spared his cousin Lot's house. We have yet to realize the power of prayer in this world. As an intercessor, the Holy Spirit will prompt you to greater levels in prayer; dimensions far beyond where you ever thought He could take you.

"Now it came to pass in those days that He went out to the mountain to pray, and continued all night in prayer to God." Luke 6:12

Jesus was our example of how we ought to pray. He was at the apex of prayer. He communed consistently with the Father; receiving the necessary instructions from God to fulfill His purpose in the earth. How many of us have labored in prayer ALL NIGHT before? Not that this is something that is required of you in particular, but there will be times when God may ask you to do so. Will you be ready? We say that we want God to use us in any way that He chooses, but are we willing to lay down our lives; our time, our families, and our wants to intercede for someone else? This was Jesus' purpose here in the earth. He was human, just as we are; He was faced with the very feelings and emotions that we are faced with in our flesh, but He overcame those temptations to fulfill the will of His Father. This is what God desires of us, His Sons, in the earth to this day.

God knows that the sacrifice and discipline of an intercessor is not by any means an easy one, but as you submit yourself to the Holy Spirit's leading, He will strengthen you greatly for the assignment. I can attest to the many nights that the Holy Spirit woke me from my sleep to intercede. In the beginning, I was on fire for the Lord. I would awaken and just go right into prayer. I would pray and intercede for hours on end; sometimes, ushering in the dawn of the day. It was amazing to me how I would labor all night in prayer and get right into the day energized and refreshed as if I had a full night's rest. God can and will sustain you in your assignment. If you are submitting to the vision, He has to supply the provision for it, no matter what that may be. He is a God that stands over His Word to perform it. He just needs a "body" in the earth to carry it out! Glory to God!

As time progressed, I found myself hearing so very much from the Holy Spirit. I was receiving instructions to carry out for Him daily and my walk with the Lord went to another level. It was such that every morning around 3:00am, the Holy Spirit would awaken me for my assignment. There were times when He gave me specific instructions to pray for; there were times where I just spoke in my heavenly language all night, and then there were times where I would just lay on my face; still and quiet. Whatever it is that may transpire out of this assignment, it is your obedience in getting up that moves the Lord. Is this an easy assignment? No, but if you are willing to take it on, God will make a way for you to overcome the challenges of the assignment.

"Be anxious for nothing, but in everything by prayer and supplication, with thanksgiving, let your requests be made known to God; and the peace of God, which surpasses all understanding, will guard your hearts and mind through Christ Jesus." Philippians 4:6-7

83

There would not be a time when I did not receive some kind of insight or revelation into a situation. It was only after a while of being obedient in meeting with the Father every morning, that I found myself not hearing "clearly" from Him. I thought that I had done something wrong; I thought that God took the 'assignment' away from me for whatever reason. I struggled with this for several weeks, until the Holy Spirit shared with me that there is a time when we will feel as if He has withdrawn Himself from us, but this is a time when our faithfulness and obedience to intercede will be tested. God desires for us to live a lifestyle of intercession; where we will see a situation and just intercede with the boldness that He has placed on the inside of us.

I don't know about you, but I am one who stays up to date on world news. It never fails me when I turn on the news that the Holy Spirit will prompt me to intercede for something or someone. As an intercessor, your 'inner man' will be quickened, or prompted more often than not. Never brush these instances off as just a coincidence because in God there are no coincidences. If you are a born-again believer and filled with the Holy Spirit, He will speak to you. You may hear people tell you that it is just your instincts, but we know that without the Holy Spirit, we cannot and will not "hear" from God. It has nothing in the world to do with us, but it is ALL ABOUT HIM!

You will find that the Holy Spirit will speak to you to intercede for people and situations that you may not want to intercede for or may not agree with. Again, it is not about you, but about His plans being fulfilled in the earth through you. You are only a vessel that He will use to accomplish His mission. I remember when the United States military invaded Iraq for the second time; 2003. My husband was already overseas and I was to meet him in a few months. I was standing in my best friend's kitchen and the television was on. I saw a breaking news update and there it was; bombs being dropped and it just seemed like it would never end. My spirit was "thrust" into intercession. I am not sure exactly how long the actual onset of the bombing took place, but I stayed in intercession for quite some time. I was travailing in prayer to the point where when I opened my eyes, my best friend's son was down on his knees praying with me. I was so moved by this display of God's power, that even a child felt the presence of God's Spirit in that room.

No matter if you are the only one interceding in a prayer meeting; no matter if you are the only one who will stand up and intercede on behalf of the nations, God will honor your prayers and He is faithful to answer them as well. People may think that you are crazy because of your passion to pray, but this should not be our concern. When you know that your assignment is to intercede, everyone and everything that can cause you to become distracted must be removed from your life. I was told by several people, including our man of God, that I better get ready to lose a lot of 'friendships', if you will. They shared with me that even in this stage of ministry, people would look at me and scoff because they do not understand what intercession is all about anyway. Not that they could not understand if they just availed themselves, but that they would just not even try to understand; therefore, they would persecute me for just being obedient.

There are people in the house of the Lord who are saved, but have yet to experience being born-again believers. There is a difference. Our man of God taught a series on this subject and it truly opened my eyes up to why I became so frustrated with others who did not seem to get what I was getting from the Word of God. He shared with us that the Word is for everyone, but not everyone comes to the house with the right motives, so many will miss it, but when they see you prospering from it, they become envious and even upset with you. This should not be your concern because God is no respecter of persons. (Acts 10:34) You cannot allow their disobedience to interfere with your obedience. You cannot be ashamed of your faithfulness in obeying the Spirit of God in prayer. In your faithfulness and obedience, you are shining light on others' disobedience, so this makes them uncomfortable, even to the point of conviction. This is what God wants you to do.

"Let your light so shine before men, that they may see your good works and GLORIFY your Father in heaven." Matthew 5:16(emphasis mine)

Now this should never be done with the wrong motive in your heart. Your faithfulness alone will bring conviction. You do not have to tell anyone that they are being disobedient. I believe that this is one of the Body of Christ's biggest issues with unbelievers. Instead of letting our "light shine" in their midst, we are condemning them to the point where they do not even want to step foot near the house of the Lord. We need to focus on ourselves and allow the Holy Spirit to do His job.

There was another instance where the Holy Spirit prompted me to pray, but this time, it was specific. He urged me to intercede for Saddam Hussein. Now, being in a military family, many would call me crazy or better yet, call me a traitor. My own husband is in the military, but he does not come before my Father and the will of God for my life. My duty and responsibility is to pray. I immediately obeyed the voice of the Holy Spirit. I did this for a while, praying for his salvation and to come into the knowledge of Christ. Now I could not have done this without first being a born-again believer, as we discussed earlier. When God desires for us to intercede for someone; He desires for His heart to be released into the situation. This cannot be done if you do not have a genuine desire in your heart for this person to be saved or even kept from harm. I, in and of myself, could not understand why I was so emotional when I prayed for this man. I cried so deeply for his salvation. Every time that I would see the news of him about to be hanged, my heart would ache for him. My husband asked me one time why I was so deeply moved and I shared this with him. No matter how he responded, I still had to let my light shine before him; I had to still be about my Father's business.

"And He said to them, 'Why did you seek Me? Did you not know that I must be about My Father's business?" Luke 2:49

In this instance, I did not see my prayers answered in the way that I thought they would be answered. I believed it with all of my heart and I had great faith that he would live and become a witness for other Muslims, but this did not happen. Do I know if he received Jesus into his heart before he died? No, but this did not stop me from being obedient and to continue interceding.

As intercessors, you not only have a responsibility to pray and intercede, but as we saw earlier, your character must be found in good standing with those outside; whether they be in the house of the Lord or not. We have a responsibility to show them God's heart for His people. When they see you committed and faithful in prayer and your prayers being answered and God moving mightily in your life, it will persuade them to seek God on a higher level.

Now I must share with you that just because you are hearing from the Holy Spirit and interceding greatly for the Lord, this does not mean that you are free from being tempted by satan. In fact, because he knows who you are in prayer, he will target you and try to move you out of the position of intercession. We saw from the last chapter that holiness is essential in the life of an intercessor. We found that in its simplest meaning, holiness is self-control. One way to control oneself is to possess discipline. If you are not disciplined in every area of your life, satan will try and creep in and stop the flow of information from the Father to you. Is this possible? Yes because God does not just show up if you have not spent quality time in His Presence. If satan has tempted you in the area of your sleep and caused you to miss those "meetings" with the Holy Spirit, then you have become disobedient. We think being disobedient is not a sin, but in the life of a born-again believer, it is just that.

I have been tempted by satan in this very area. As I said earlier, the Holy Spirit would awaken me every morning around 3:00am. As time passed, I had many new things that God had placed in my hands to be responsible over. My time was being shifted to many different things and I found myself so very tired and when that time came for me to meet with the Holy Spirit; I would be so tired that I would just fall right back to sleep. When I woke up in the morning I would be convicted because I knew that if I had disciplined myself accordingly, I would have not missed that important time. I had to come to a point where the Word of God and my prayer life was the most important thing to me. I had to set aside everything else and make this my first priority. How do you do this? Discipline! You must set aside the first part of your day for the Lord. You must seek Him first.

"But seek first the kingdom of God and His righteousness, and all these things shall be added to you." Matthew 6:33

There are differing forms of prayer in the life of an intercessor. As we discussed earlier, we have that intimate one on one prayer time between us and God. This builds you up individually and allows intimacy between you and the Father. We also covered the use of our heavenly language in the instances when we are not given clarity to intercede. This allows insight and promptings from the Holy Spirit, being that He knows what to pray when we do not. The next area I will touch upon is an area that most people do not associate themselves with and that is in the area of weeping and travailing in prayer.

I always thought that I had issues because I was always crying, whether it was in prayer, worship, or just hearing the Word of God. There were times when I would beat myself up because I could not understand why I kept weeping in these services. I threw myself into the word of God and from there; I found my answer. The Holy Spirit led me to Jeremiah. I read from the beginning to the very end of this book and I found myself in the course of this book about the "Weeping Prophet". We must understand that the one who weeps is the true servant of God, because that servant understands the hurt in the heart of God. Once we begin to weep at the brokenness of our world, God will move on behalf of it.

Again, when we look back at Chapter 1, we have to have the heart of God when it comes to His people. We have to have a love for the lost of this world. Our heart should be so in tune with the heart of God that what hurts God; hurts us, as His servants. The prophet Jeremiah consistently displayed a heart that bore the burdens of God for His people. Even though he was prophesying certain judgment to a hard-hearted people, he still prayed earnestly for them to come to a place of repentance and to turn their heart back to God. This should be the prayer of the intercessor in this hour. Jeremiah cried out to the God of heaven on behalf of this rebellious people. Can you imagine how frustrated Jeremiah must have been to continue wholeheartedly praying for a people who, from an outward view, did not look as if they were ever going to change?

We were once those rebellious people. How long did it take us to change our ways and turn our hearts to God? This is the position that we, as intercessors, are to take; the road that the prophet Jeremiah took. Although he was given an assignment to prophesy to the people of Jerusalem, as well as Judah, and was obedient to give the message of God, he hurt on the inside for them and held a passionate belief that they could change; he held hope in his heart for God's people; he wept and lamented for them.

"I will take up a weeping and wailing for the mountains, And for the dwelling places of the wilderness a lamentation, Because they are burned up, So that no one can pass through; Nor can men hear the voice of the cattle. Both the birds of the heavens and the beasts have fled; They are gone." Jeremiah 9:10

I found myself in the beginning of my interceding very frustrated, as Jeremiah was. I would lay awake many nights standing in the gap for certain individuals and it just seemed as if they were never going to get it right? I have to say, there were several times that I wanted to just give up, but the Spirit of God moved so heavily upon me and took me back to my time of rebellion, where others prayed and interceded for me to come back to the Lord. I know where I was in the world and I know how much pain and heartache I was in, so I take that experience and intercede for others the way that I know I would want others to intercede for me.

Weeping is defined as expressing grief, sorrow, or any overwhelming emotion by shedding tears. We should feel sorrow when we look out around the world and see the chaos and turmoil that it is in. We cannot brush under the rug the atrocities that are taking place among the nations, while we sit back and live our "so-called" perfect lives. Jeremiah saw the great tumult that Israel was in and made it his life's goal to cry out to God on their behalf. There have been times when the Lord would have me on my face in tears. Several of these times, I did not even know why I was weeping, but afterwards, He would reveal the purpose behind why my spirit was prompted to weep.

Now many may ask the question, "Do you just begin weeping?" Absolutely not. This is not something that you prepare for. This is not a show or an act, but a leading of the Holy Spirit to reveal the Father's heart in a particular situation. The times when this has occurred for me have been after spending intimate time in worship and in great times of intercession. When you enter into the Holy of Holies and "see" the heart of God, He reveals to you the things that are on His heart. He reveals to us what to intercede for in the earth, as He, The Lord Himself, sits on the right hand of God interceding for us.

"It is Christ who died, and furthermore is also risen, who is even at the right hand of God, who also makes intercession for us." Romans 8:34b

God's heart breaks when His people are not living the lives that He created for them to live. His mercy and His grace abound for us greatly, but there are still times when we do not hear His voice of warning, so He will speak to those who offer up themselves freely through intercession. When God desires to reach someone in the earth realm to do great things for Him and they have yet to "see" it, He will begin to reveal to the intercessors His will for them. Depending upon the receptiveness of the individual, this very well may determine whether God will send a weeping into your spirit for this person. Again, not too many intercessors move in this realm for several reasons. First, they have not caught the heart of God for His people. Second, they are too concerned with their own agendas that they have lost sight of His agenda, and finally, they are too ashamed that others will see them and call them crazy.

Well, I have chosen to be none of the above. God has placed a great burden in my heart to weep for His people and the nations and to intercede on their behalf. My prayer is that all of you whom He has called to intercede, that you will accept the call and allow the Spirit of God to lead you however He chooses to lead you, to draw His people back to Him.

There are also several times in scripture where we see a "crying out" for the people of God. We know that Jeremiah was considered the weeping prophet because of his heart for the people of God, as well as his knowing that without God, he could do nothing. His dependence was fully on the Lord, regardless of the fact that he was reluctant to do what the Lord asked Him to do at times. There are times when God will send a wave through your spirit of crying out! These are times when imminent danger is near or when someone is about to enter into a dangerous situation and the Holy Spirit will send for that cry to combat the plans of satan over that individual's life.

I have heard countless testimonies of saints who were prompted to cry out to the Lord on behalf of individuals who were in such dire circumstances from drug addiction to thoughts of taking their own lives. The Holy Spirit will call upon you at various times to intercede by way of crying out because this rocks the very foundations of hell to let go of God's property! The power in your voice and the love in your heart send shockwaves through the kingdom of darkness. This is a powerful form of intercession because it takes you moving out of your comfort zone of praying, into an act of doing something for someone else. This moves you into action!

"Their heart cried out to the Lord, "O wall of the daughter of Zion, Let tears run down like a river day and night; Give yourself no relief; Give your eyes no rest." Lamentations 2:18

This type of intercession is the way that most parents cry out for their lost children. Whether they are on drugs or in the streets, and there seems to be no hope for them, you will see the parents cry out to God to save their children and bring them home. This should be the same for the intercessor. No matter who it is that God is asking you to cry out for, you must see them as God sees them and love them as God loves them, and let out a cry that will bombard the gates of hell to let that soul go. As I stated in Chapter one, you must have a burden in your heart for the lost of this world.

The last aspect of prayer that we will discuss is in the area of travailing. Travailing is defined as painfully difficult or burdensome work; toil. Ok, we already came to the conclusion that there will not be too many intercessors who will weep on behalf of God's people, so the next question is, "How many are willing to travail for God's people?" Painfully difficult; burdensome work? Who is willing to go to work for eight hours a day, come home and prepare dinner or finish up last minute work, get the kids bathed and put in bed, spend some quality time with your spouse, finally get to sleep, and here the Holy Spirit is, waking you up at 3:00am to travail in prayer for someone you may not even know, or for something that you have no idea about?

Come on now, how many of us are ready to commit to something like this? How many of us are going to accept such an assignment from the Lord? I am here to tell you that it is not by any means and easy assignment if you are looking to fulfill it by yourself, but when you allow the Holy Spirit to lead and direct you, you will begin to see the benefits of such an assignment. Travailing is associated with the actual pains of childbirth. When a woman enters into the travailing stage of childbirth, she bears down with all of her strength focused on the lower part of her body and with all of her might, she pushes down. Now the first, second, or even third time might not produce what it is that she is looking for, but this does not stop her from taking a few deep breaths to prepare for the next phase of travailing. She will continue this until she sees the "fruit" of her labor. Glory to God!

"He shall see the travail of his soul, and be satisfied: by his knowledge shall my righteous servant justify many; for he shall bear their iniquities." Isaiah 53:11, KJV

Here is an example of Jesus' sacrifice for us and how, though the pain and anguish of His own soul was great, it was worth it to Him that many others would enter into salvation. As you travail in prayer for others, it does take a toll on your physical body because you are going through a "burdensome" task of ushering someone else into the Kingdom of God. It is just as that mother who is ushering that unborn child into the world, but this is a spiritual birth. There have been instances where I travailed in prayer for people and situations and sometimes it was hours that I stayed in this realm. My stomach muscles hurt because of the force with which I prayed; my throat hurt because of the outcry of my voice, and I physically could do nothing but go to sleep afterwards because I was physically drained.

You will know when something has 'come forth' in intercession. You feel the release, if you will, of people or situations. Just as that baby begins to "crown" in the mother's womb, she knows that there is no turning back. This child is at that crucial stage of entering into the world. If the mother stops pushing or pushes too soon, great danger can take place for that child. The same holds true in intercession. Once you feel that "crowning", or climax in intercession, take a few deep breaths and press forward until you feel the release in the spirit realm. Do not try to rush the Spirit of God, but avail yourself to His leading. Allow Him to guide you through that thing and give Him His office space; you are just a body, or vessel, that He uses to cause His plans to enter into the earth realm.

*"For I have heard a voice as of a woman in **travail**, and the anguish as of her that bringeth forth her first child, the voice of the daughter of Zion, that bewaileth herself, that spreadeth her hands, saying, Woe is me now! for my soul is wearied because of murderers."* *Jeremiah4:31, KJV (emphasis mine)*

You should be so distraught at the sinfulness in the world and the rebellion of the people, that you are willing to travail in prayer on their behalf. Again, this type of prayer is not being utilized by many in the church today. We saw from even the Old Testament days that there were usually only a few prophets that were obedient to carry out God's assignment on their lives. These prophets were truly concerned with the disobedience of the people to the point that they went above and beyond their duty to release a word, by crying, weeping, and travailing in prayer for them.

Many within the church get to a point where they feel as if they have done enough to try and help others. They feel as if the people they are praying for could care less, so they say, "Why should I waste my time praying for them? Why should I sacrifice my time and my rest to labor all night, travailing in prayer for someone who seems like they don't even want to change?" Hmmm. Have you ever thought that someone possibly did this for you? Have you ever stopped to think that you could be dead today if someone had not hearkened to the Holy Spirit's leading to intercede on your behalf? The word selfish should in no way be a part of an intercessor's life and cannot, if you are truly an intercessor. There is nothing more selfless than to intercede for others, especially through travailing in the spirit realm for their release into the Kingdom of God.

*"When birth pangs signaled it was time to be born, Ephraim was too stupid to come out of the womb. When the passage into life opened up, he didn't show". 14a: "**Shall I intervene** and pull them into life? **Shall I snatch** them from a certain death?" Hosea 13:13-14a, MSG (emphasis mine)*

How great is your desire to see a soul released from satan's grip and ushered into the Kingdom of God? How heavy is the burden in your heart to intercede for the lost and dying of this world? How great is your passion to see God's plans manifest in the earth realm? The answers to these questions will determine the mantle of intercession upon your life; it will determine what your calling and purpose is as it relates to the ministry of intercession.

The next area of discipline that we will discuss is in the area of fasting. There are many different ways to fast and we do not all fast in the same manner or even for the same reasons. The first and most important thing that I will say about fasting is this, "Never look at what someone else is doing as your guide to fasting." Fasting has to be primarily an individual experience. We must be seeking the counsel of God for what it is that He desires of us and not doing what He has told someone else to do. As we sacrifice our own bodies or our own pleasures, we are displaying a disciplined lifestyle where the Spirit of God can come in and pour His will into our lives. We know that Jesus not only displayed a lifestyle of prayer, but He also was disciplined in the area of fasting.

"And when He had fasted forty days and forty nights, afterwards He was hungry." Matthew 4:2

In this portion of scripture, Jesus is being tempted by satan in the very three areas that we spoke of earlier; the lust of the flesh, the lust of the eyes, and the pride of life. He was a man, just as we are, but

He overcame those temptations through the crucifying of His flesh as He fasted. We saw that as soon as he came out of the wilderness, satan was right there to tempt Him in the very area that He may have been weak in at that moment. The scripture says, "afterwards he was hungry." No matter how faithful you are to fast, you have to be mindful of your own personal weaknesses and guard yourself against the enemy's schemes.

Fasting is defined as a period of such abstention (withholding or abstaining) or self-denial. When you deny yourself and your own personal desires for a moment to seek the Father's face, you will be able to withstand the enemy's tactics. Now just because you fast, do not think that satan will leave you alone because he will more than likely try and tempt you, being that you are in a vulnerable state. You cannot just fast and not replace the void with the Word of God, because it is the Word that will sustain you. Not applying the Word of God to your time of fasting nullifies why you are even fasting in the first place. You are seeking instructions through fasting, so allow Him to speak to you, not only through His Spirit, but also through His Word.

We see throughout the Bible instances where people fasted so that they could hear clearly from God. The majority of these fastings were directly from food. Now we can fast from television, internet, and so forth, but to deny your flesh through fasting from food is a practice that brought great changes into the lives of those in the Bible. We saw from the prophet Daniel how this became more than a one-time experience for him; it became a lifestyle for Daniel.

"But Daniel purposed in his heart that he would not defile himself with the portion of the king's delicacies, nor with the wine which he drank; therefore he requested of the chief of the eunuchs that he might not defile himself." Daniel 1:8

Daniel made clear in the beginning that this was something that he had already been accustomed to; he had prior knowledge that this would benefit him. He told the man to prove them for ten days; not giving them the meat or strong drink and to see how they would fair, in comparison to those who partook of the food and drink. After those ten days, Daniel and his friends faired much better than the others, so they were given pulse to eat, instead of the regular meat and drink. Pulse is defined as the edible seeds of certain leguminous plants, such as peas, beans, or lentils. So we see that Daniel fasted on a specific diet that benefited him greatly.

"As for these four young men, God gave them knowledge and skill in all literature and wisdom; and Daniel had understanding in all visions and dreams." Daniel 1:17

When we fast, we give God room to pour His wisdom and understanding into our lives. When you set yourself apart from others and fast, you are giving God a reason to show Himself strong and mighty over your life. Everyone wants to hear a word from God, but not everyone is willing to do what it takes to get that word. It pleases God when we deny ourselves and take up His cause, instead of our own. The insight given to intercessors is greatly impacted by the degree of fasting in their lives. Whenever you give up something; you will always gain something greater. God sent Jesus, His Only Son to die on the cross for us, but in return, not only did He get His Son back, but many sons to follow. Glory to God!

Fasting may not look beneficial while you are going through, but in the end, you will absolutely see the results of your sacrifice, as well as your obedience. Just as in intercession, fasting is not a widespread activity within the church. Many people say that they fast, and some do to the point that is comfortable to them, but the selfless act of fasting to hear from the Almighty God is not common amongst the majority. As I said earlier, there are differing fasts that we can enter into and many reasons why we do so, but we have to make sure that we are fasting for the right reasons and with the right motives.

"We have fasted before you!' they say. 'Why aren't you impressed? We have been very hard on ourselves, and you don't even notice it!" v.4- "I will tell you why!" I respond. "It's because you are fasting to please yourselves.

Even while you fast, you keep oppressing your workers. What good is fasting when you keep on fighting and quarreling? This kind of fasting will never get you anywhere with me." Isaiah 58:3-4, NLT

There are some who put on a show to obtain benefits, without having a heart that is focused on obtaining answers and instructions from the Lord. These are they who even while they say they are fasting, go about their day to day business with anger, strife, bitterness, and greed still in their hearts. God says that you may as well not fast at all if this is the route that you are going to take. As we saw in Chapter Four, Holiness is essential in the life of the intercessor and if you possess holiness, this type of behavior will be far from you. When you allow yourself to be disciplined by the Word of God in every one of these areas, it leads you to another dimension in your walk with the Lord. You will possess a strong sense of maturity, and through your experiences in prayer and fasting; God will release a greater level of authority into your hands.

Make prayer and fasting a priority in your day to day walk with God and watch Him move greatly through you in the area of intercession. The same way that a fish needs water or a plant needs sunlight to survive; an intercessor being used by the Lord to move mountains in the earth needs a lifestyle of consistent prayer and fasting. We had the best example in the life of Jesus in the earth. Let us purpose to imitate Him and impact this world for God. You are on assignment. Will you answer the call?

❦IN HIS IMAGE,

LIKENESS & NATURE❦

*"Then God said, "Let Us make man in OUR IMAGE, accord-
ing to OUR LIKENESS; let them have dominion over the fish of the
sea, over the birds of the air, and over the cattle, over all the earth and
over every creeping thing that creeps on the earth."*

Genesis 1:26(emphasis mine)

*"Therefore, since we are the OFFSPRING of God, we ought
not to think that the DIVINE NATURE is like gold or silver or stone,
something shaped by art and man's devising."*

Acts 17:29 (emphasis mine)

All of the previous chapters dealt with the many ways in which
we, as intercessors, are to live and conduct ourselves in our day to day
lives. Once you get these basic foundations down and begin to operate
in them on a consistent basis, then you will begin to walk in the image,
likeness, and nature of God. God created us in His image and in His
likeness for the purpose of having dominion on the earth. If you are an
intercessor, then you must possess these vital characteristics of God.

You will not obtain them all at one time, but it is absolutely a process in which you are taught by the Spirit of God; how you are to move in them effectively. The image of God, as described in the Genesis one text, is that of resembling. You must look like God. We know that in Genesis 1:26, it says, "in Our image". We know from this text that this represents the Godhead; the Father, the Son, and the Holy Spirit. We were created in His very image; we resemble Him. When we encounter anyone, we should look, sound, walk, talk, and act like the One who created us; God Himself.

Our pastor began teaching a timely message entitled: The Image, Likeness, and Nature of God[6] and it opened my eyes greatly to how God desires to use us in the earth realm. Until we find out who we are, we will not operate in the earth according to that picture or image. We must understand that we have to go higher in our own thinking to understand how we are able to be the image of God on earth. This cannot become a reality to you if you only accept Jesus as your Savior and refuse to accept Christ as your developer. There are greater levels of revelation that the Lord is trying to get us to see, but if all we are looking for is to get to heaven, why would He pour out this revelation into our lives?

"and have put on the new man who is renewed in knowledge according to the image of Him who created him," Colossians 3:10

You must accept who He says you are and not who "Mom, Dad, brother, sister, or friend" tells you that you are. You have to obtain knowledge in His Word of who He created you to be and once you seek it out, you will find that you were created in His very image. If you allow man to tell you who you are, then you will only accept what they say, instead of the very One who created you. If you allow this, your witness will be a watered down version of the truth and you will not be effective to reach a lost people; let alone stand in the gap as the image of God in the earth, to produce results in their lives.

People ought to know who you are and whose you are. They should see the "resemblance" and know that you are a man or woman of God who obtains results from the Lord. They should see a consistency in your life as one who is committed, submitted, and obedient to the voice of God and to the leading of His Holy Spirit. If they do not see this operating in your life, they will not know how they should look. You are to be a "living epistle", if you will, in others' lives. The word has to become flesh and dwell on the inside of you, (John 1:14) for it to be effective in the life of another. Do not allow the enemy to slander your name or discredit what God has foreordained for your life.

"And He said to them, "Whose image and inscription is this?"
Matthew 22:20

Do others know whose image and inscription you carry? Do they, without a shadow of a doubt, know that you are a son of God and that you bear resemblance to the one true God? If others cannot tell the difference, how do you think satan can? We have to be the express image of God in this earth to be able to stand against the tricks and schemes of the enemy. We have to know who and Whose we are, in order to be effective in the ministry of intercession.

Do you know Whose you are? Have you taken the time out to find in His Word what He thinks about you and who He says you are? Again, we find so many times in the lives of Christians that the reason why they are not prospering and why they still continue to ask so many questions about their lives is because they have failed to read, study, and meditate on the Word of God. If we honestly did this, as we are supposed to, then we would know that we are the very image of God and that He created us to resemble Him. Once you find out that you are made in His image, then your entire perception of yourself, as well as the world, changes. You will begin to see things as God Himself sees them. You will no longer view life as just a space in time that once it is gone, it is over, but you will see that God created you with a purpose and in that purpose, you bear His image.

"But we all, with unveiled face, beholding as in a mirror the glory of the Lord, are being transformed into the same image from glory to glory, just as by the Spirit of the Lord." 2 Corinthians 3:18

This is a progressive text. We are being transformed daily into the image of God our Father. The old is being removed and the new is being implanted into our lives every day. As we continue on this path, God is molding us into the very image that He created us in; free from all outside influence. As you see a baby being transformed daily in every aspect of his life, from his speech to his appearance, the same is true for us as believers. Each morning that we wake up, we should be able to look into the mirror and see a change in our lives. We should see every day something different in our lives and if we do not, then we have not been in His presence. When you enter into the presence of the Lord; truly enter in, you cannot come out the same. The way you walk, the way you talk, the way you dress, the way you see, the way you hear, and the way you love will change once you see the image of God overshadowing your entire life.

What seemed important before in your life will become meaningless. What bothered you before will no longer bother you. What caused you to "snap" before will no longer be an issue to you. You will take on the image of God in every aspect of your life. You will begin to look like Him. Jesus was the express image of God in this earth. No matter what others did to Him, He knew that He and His Father were one and because He knew that, He chose to "look" like His Father in every area of His life. His present circumstances did not change who God created Him to be, but gave Him an opportunity to reveal the glory of God, or the image of God, to those who did not know Him. God created you from His wisdom. He knew ahead of time how you would look, where you would be born, and what gift you would operate in on earth. He knew who you would be before He even created you. Glory to God!

"For whom He foreknew, He also predestined to be conformed to the image of His Son, that He might be the firstborn among many brethren." Romans 8:29

The firstborn among many brethren; God wanted sons in the earth to represent Him and Jesus was the frontrunner in this plan. Jesus would always say in the word that when you saw Him, you saw the Father as well, because He and the Father are one. This is how others should see you, just as they see Jesus and just as they see God. You are the image of God in the earth realm.

The likeness in Genesis 1:26, also represents the character of resembling, but moves on further by showing us that we are a model of Him, the shape of Him, and the fashion of Him. This scripture is a progressive scripture in the sense that we move from resembling Him, to taking on the shape and fashion of God Himself. As you seek God in greater ways, He will reveal Himself in greater ways. God will only reveal Himself to the extent of how you seek Him. This is powerful. We expect Him to give us great revelation and answer our prayers, but we refuse to seek Him with all of our heart, so that we can become like Him in every area of our lives.

This is where most Christians miss it. We want the power of God to operate in our lives, but we are unwilling or afraid to allow the power to dwell in us because we do not want to let go of our former likeness in the world; to be transformed into the likeness of God.

"And do not be conformed to this world, but be transformed by the renewing of your mind, that you may prove what is that good and acceptable and perfect will of God." Romans 12:2

Once you allow the word of God and the Holy Spirit to renew that old mindset, then you will become fashioned like God. You will begin to not only look like Him, but you will begin to act like Him. Have you heard the saying, "Your actions speak louder than your words?" You can say all day long that you are a son of God, but if your actions are not displaying this confession, then it is useless and ineffective. The likeness of God takes it a little further from resembling. When you resemble someone, you share a few characteristics, but it ends there. Resembling is representative of the thirty fold principle in the Bible, but the likeness represents the sixty fold. However you see yourself will determine the expectation that you will have from God. If you just see yourself as resembling God, then you will skim the top of the water and quickly step back because it will become too overwhelming for you; being that you do not see yourself as more than just a glimpse of God in the earth. What you receive from

God will be minimal and it will frustrate you because you will feel as if you are obtaining more in the world than you are receiving in the Kingdom of God. This is why we see so many Christians who are frustrated in their walk with God, because they have not moved past salvation. God has greater for you if you are willing to receive it, but it must start with you first.

The likeness of God shows us the sixty fold dimension of blessing, if you will. You are now beginning to act out what you have heard God say that you are. You are now moving out into the water, even treading upon that water. You feel more secure and you feel as if you have experienced enough in your walk where you can step out in faith and begin interceding for others, as opposed to just asking God to bless you. Now when you felt as if you resembled God, you could not grasp, with that thirty fold thinking, that you could go beyond just praying for you and your immediate family. This type of mindset tells you that yes, you are saved and are going to heaven, but anything else past that it unattainable for you.

There are many in the body of Christ that fit into the thirty fold category and this is a sad reality. They never move past the salvation stage and as our man of God quotes, they are "frustrated, disillusioned, and hard to get along with." Now the ones that do make it past this stage are truly the ones in the most danger in my eyes. They know that they have gone higher in their level of thinking and are seeing fruit abound to their accounts, but they stop here believing that they have arrived. This is the stage where pride can fester in a believer's life, as well as in the life of an intercessor. You are hearing from God and you are stepping out on what you have heard by taking action to intercede. You do so and you begin to see the results of your obedience, but you get comfortable right here and refuse to seek God on a higher level. Through your faithfulness in intercession, others see you and respect you and know you to be one who will stand in the gap if need be. Be mindful and very watchful of this stage in your walk, because you appear to others as having it all together, but in reality, you are right in the middle of a process that is shifting you to a greater dimension. This is when you appear to be something that you are not. This is the kind of ground the enemy loves to intrude upon.

"Like the appearance of a rainbow in a cloud on a rainy day, so was the appearance of the brightness all around it. This was the appearance of the likeness of the glory of the Lord." Ezekiel 1:28

The word likeness in this text denotes comparison. We saw that image has a connotation of resemblance and that says, "You kind of look like Him, but I am not sure." Likeness in this text says, "Well, it appears that you are like Him and I can compare the things that you do with what I saw Him do, but I am still not one hundred percent sure." As you begin to take on the likeness of God, others should be able to compare you with your Father. They should not only hear you saying that you are a son of God, but also they should be able to see you acting like Him. This is not automatic when we are born into this world. We saw from Genesis Chapter 1 that Adam and Eve were created in the image and likeness of God, but once they compromised that relationship, they no longer possessed this character, but they began to take on their own image and their own likeness.

"And Adam lived one hundred and thirty years, and begot a son in his own likeness, after his image, and named him Seth." Genesis 5:3

The image and likeness that we possess should not be that of our own. When it comes to the ministry of intercession, we cannot and should not view things outside of how God sees them. We are to view people and situations as God does. Even though we were born into this world of sin; taking on the likeness of our earthly fathers, it does not stop here. You do not have to accept this and live the rest of your lives outside of the likeness of your heavenly Father. God gave us a plan of redemption and restoration through His Son Jesus Christ. God desires not only to save us, but to restore us back to the original purpose for creating us in the beginning.

Our lives should reflect who it is that we are serving. If you are serving God, then you should look to others as just that; the One whom you serve. This is a vital point in the life of a believer. Our entire purpose in the church is to come and be transformed from that old likeness, renewed in our minds, and then, to be sent out into the world to reveal the "new" person. Once others see you changed from the person that they knew before, they see hope for themselves. If you call yourself a believer or a Christian and you are still talking and acting like you were in the world, why would those around you who are not saved want to come into the Kingdom of God? What example are you showing them? Why would they want to trade what they have in the world for what you call great when you are walking around broke, frustrated, and unhappy?

We must make up in our minds that the world has nothing to offer us anymore. We must know that the Word of God is true from the beginning and that all that is written in it is for our benefit. We must make up in our minds that we are created in His image and in His likeness and that what He says is ours; is ours! In the life of an intercessor, this is absolutely paramount. If you do not believe that you are created in His image and likeness, then how are you going to come boldly before His throne of grace on behalf of others and situations? How are you going to stand on the Word of God in intercession if you do not believe that were created to be just like Him? For an intercessor to flow in this ministry, you have to know that God will only stand in agreement with Himself in the earth. Glory to God!

You must allow the Word of God to become you and the Spirit of God to overshadow you in every area of your life. Once this becomes a part of you, then you will begin to take on the true nature of God. Nature is defined as the instincts or inherent tendencies directing conduct, or the moral state as unaffected by grace. The Hebrew word for nature is *lach*, which means to be new, fresh, or unused. The Greek word for nature is Genesis, which is translated as nativity. If we compare these definitions, we see that the original intent of God was for our nature to be as He was; unaffected by grace, or how it was supposed to be before Jesus was sent to restore it. When we look at the Greek translation, we see that our nature is our nativity. Nativity is defined as birth, especially the place, conditions, or circumstances of being born. It is also defined as the birth of Jesus. Genesis is the beginning and just how God created us in the beginning, is how He desires for us to end up.

When the earth was created, God spoke what He wanted into the earth realm. He created the heavens, the earth, the sun, moon, and stars, the land and all of the creatures that would dwell therein, the waters and every moving creature, the birds of the air, the cattle, beasts, and every creeping thing after its own kind. Then, God created man. Now man was not created with the nature of the cattle, the beasts, or the creeping things of the earth, but he was created in the image of God.

"God spoke: "Let us make human beings in our image, make them reflecting our nature." Genesis 1:26 (MSG)

God's nature was released into the earth realm through the creation of Adam and Eve. He desired for His original character to occupy the earth through the formation of the man and woman. But we know from Genesis Chapter Three that the nature that walked through the Garden in the cool of the day in constant communion with the Creator was intercepted and cut off through the conniving and deceitful lure of the enemy. At this very point in scripture, the true and divine nature of the man was lost. As soon as they ate, their eyes were opened to the reality that they had disobeyed their Creator; they were now naked; exposed. Verse six of Chapter Three shows us how satan tempted Eve.

"So when the woman saw that the tree was good for food (the lust of the flesh), that it was pleasant to the eyes (the lust of the eyes), and a tree desirable to make one wise (the pride of life), she took of its fruit and ate. She also gave to her husband with her, and he ate." Genesis 3:6, (emphasis mine)

The enemy can and will only tempt the believer in three areas, and these were the very three areas that he fell victim to himself. The nature of the enemy is to kill, steal, and to destroy. (John 10:10) He saw how God created man. He himself was an angel and he desired to be like God. When he found out that God had created a man in His image and likeness that would rule in the earth, satan became livid. He was cast out of heaven for his rebellion to be like God, so he wanted to persuade the "new" man to do the same. At the point of rebellion, the sinful nature, or the nature of satan, was released into man.

"by which have been given to us exceedingly great and precious promises, that through these you may be partakers of the divine nature, having escaped the corruption that is in the world through lust." 2 Peter 1:4

It says in this particular scripture that we may be partakers of the divine nature of God. The only way for us to receive this divine nature again is to do just what the scripture says, "Escape the corruption that is in this world". We learned through the earlier chapters, ways to prepare ourselves to receive this nature for the ministry of intercession; from allowing ourselves to love others as God loves, receiving the free gift of the Holy Spirit, knowing when to speak and when not to speak, developing a lifestyle of holiness, and disciplining our lives through prayer and fasting. This seems like a very strict lifestyle to lead and to some, it may even sound impossible, but I am here to tell you that it is possible. Again, we might not always get it right, but we should be pressing toward that mark daily.

If you can look back on your life prior to salvation and see change in your life, then you are on your way; you are on the right track. I know that the nature that I possessed in the world is no where near who I am today. Through the power of God's Word and the leading of His Spirit, I am that "new creation" spoken of by Paul in Corinthians.

"Therefore, if anyone is in Christ, he is a new creation; old things have passed away; behold, all things have become new." 2 Corinthians 5:17

There goes that word again, new. If you apply all of the aforementioned areas to your life, then you cannot help but become new. You have to have a desire to change and a desire to be like God. You must want to reverence the Lord with your transformed life; giving Him honor and glory by being His example in the earth. You must know that you may be the only example that many will ever see of

God in the earth. There are so many influences in today's society of so-called role models, such as entertainers, sports stars, and so forth who claim to have a heart for the people, but who are only out for publicity and such. The word of God commands us, as the people of God, to "let your light so shine before men that they will see your good works and glorify God." (Matthew 5:16) Now as others give to the poor, build orphanages, and sponsor fundraisers for the AIDS epidemic, God is not receiving the glory, but it is going to them personally. If we are to affect this world with real change, we are to possess the nature of God in the earth and make it known to the world Who we are representing. As intercessors, this will not necessarily be how you represent the Father. There are those whom God blesses to pour financially into these very pertinent projects, but your job is a behind-the-scenes project. While others may be in the spotlight revealing God's glory; you may very well be in that prayer closet, in your local congregation, or even on the road in your car about to reach a terrible accident where God would have you go to immediately intercede.

This assignment is by far the most fulfilling assignment that I have ever received. I have seen the nature of God revealed in my life greatly since I moved to Germany. My nature now as an intercessor is to respond to the prompting of the Holy Spirit when there is a need; whether it is on the road going to church, or in the privacy of my home at 3:00am. My life is submitted to the leading of the Spirit of God and His nature is being formed in my life daily. When I see someone down or depressed, my new nature thrusts me into a state of exhortation. Everything within me wants to take this person under my wings and cover them with the love of God. When you truly develop the nature of God, you will want to share it with everyone. When you possess the divine nature of God on the inside of you, you will begin to love what God loves and hate what God hates. You will have the mind of God as you purpose to display His nature.

"Let this mind be in you which was also in Christ Jesus," Philippians 2:5

It says let, which means that it is available, but you have to want to have the mind of Christ. You have to want to bear the nature of your heavenly Father within yourself. We saw in the accounts of the disciples that these men walked daily with Jesus. They did not have to question or guess how they were supposed to act, because they had the perfect example standing right in front of them, but for many, this was still not enough to change their nature. We saw in the account of Peter, how he continued to kick against the pricks; He resisted the authority that God was trying to impart into his life through Jesus. He was considered the disciple who always had his foot in his mouth. Instead of just taking what Jesus said for face value and walking in His very nature, Peter, from time to time, reverted back to his old nature, or sinful nature.

"And the Lord said, "Simon, Simon! Indeed, Satan has asked for you, that he may sift you as wheat." Luke 22:31

Jesus was calling Peter from his former state, or his former nature. He called him Simon, instead of Peter. You will see throughout the Gospel accounts where Jesus would let the disciples know when they were rearing off course by calling them by their previous names. Because Peter was usually the one veering off, you see His name being mentioned more than any other disciple. It was not until Peter caught a revelation from God Himself before he was able to retain the nature of God inside.

"Jesus came back, "God bless you, Simon, son of Jonah! You didn't get that answer out of books or from teachers. My Father in heaven, God himself, let you in on this secret of who I really am. And now I'm going to tell you who you are, really are. You are Peter, a rock. This is the rock on which I will put together my church, a church so expansive with energy that not even the gates of hell will be able to keep it out." Matthew 16:18 (MSG)

This was the point of transformation for Peter. Jesus said to Peter, "And now I am going to tell you who you are, really are." This is powerful! We must know who we are in Christ. We cannot allow the enemy to sift us as wheat by causing us to doubt who our Father is and what it is that He has called us to do for Him. If you look back at Luke 22:31, you see that Jesus told Simon that satan had asked for him. The only reason that satan will ask God for you is if he knows that you are unaware of whom you are. Once you become planted in the reality that you are a son of God and that His nature dwells in you, you will begin to possess qualities that will have the enemy scurrying to find a way to stop you from carrying out God's plan for His Kingdom in the earth.

There are several ways that you can prepare yourself to possess the nature of God within you and to maintain this nature in a world that is lacking it. As you begin to let go of your old way of thinking, acting, and living, the Word of God will open your eyes to fresh and new revelation day by day. As you grow and mature in the Word of God and allow the Spirit of God to lead you and guide you, a lifestyle of change will take place in you. You will begin thinking, speaking, acting, and living in an entirely different way. Here are some of the ways in which you can prepare yourself to maintain the nature of God in your life.

1. Prayer & Intercession
2. Reading the Word of God
3. Studying the Word of God
4. Meditating upon the Word of God
5. Maintaining a Lifestyle of Worship
6. Abundant Giving
7. Servanthood

PRAYER & INTERCESSION

We know that prayer is considered the direct line of communication to the Father in heaven. You must have an active prayer life with the Lord and maintain this daily, in order to build yourself up and gain a solid foundation in your communion with the Father. This is the thirty fold dimension of communication between Creator and creation and should be administered daily and even throughout the day to solidify your relationship with God. Intercession is defined as an interposing or pleading on behalf of another person. Once you begin to mature in your prayer life, God will begin to prompt you through His

Holy Spirit to pray for someone else or for certain situations. This is moving out of your own petitions of need and pleading to God on behalf of someone or something else. This is considered the sixty fold dimension of communication with the Lord. God will use you mightily as you submit your will to His and stand in the gap on behalf of others. We will discuss in the next chapter what the one hundred fold dimension of prayer is.

'Therefore I exhort first of all that supplications, prayers, intercessions, and giving of thanks be made for all men," (1 Timothy 2:1)

READING THE WORD OF GOD

The only true way to develop maturity is to read the Word of God. Once you become saved, you need to be planted in a Bible teaching ministry where you can grow in the things of God. Begin by taking the scriptures that your man or woman of God teach on and develop a lifestyle of reading the Word of God. As you discipline yourself to read, God will begin to open your eyes to many things that you were not previously keen to. Now please do not try to start out reading vast amounts of scripture that will lead you to wasting precious time and coming out of the experience not retaining any of it. Start out small and begin to read what you are able to understand and as you remain consistent to this practice, God will move you out into deeper waters.

"And it shall be with him, and he shall read it all the days of his life, that he may learn to fear the LORD his God and be careful to observe all the words of this law and these statutes." (Deuteronomy 17:19)

STUDYING THE WORD OF GOD

Once you commit to read the Word of God, then you will desire to know more of what it is saying to you about your life. You will move from just reading the word to studying it out in depth. The key to studying is to stick with the main purpose for your own life and what God is saying to you through your set man or woman of God. I hear so many in the Body of Christ say that they do not know what to study. This is absurd! If you are a part of a local church and you are attending regular services, then you are hearing the Word that God has specifically designed for your life in that season. He will purposely give the set man or woman of God the word for your life and you must take that word and study it out. What I tell those who ask me how I study is to take the word that was given to you on Sunday and study that word through to their midweek message. From that message, study all the way until Sunday when the next message is taught. In this, you will know what God is saying to you at that specific time in your life and you will prosper greatly. You will grow and mature and you will begin to know who you are and what the plan for your life is and you will begin to understand what the word is saying to you.

"Study to shew thyself approved unto God, a workman that needeth not to be ashamed, rightly dividing the word of truth." (2 Timothy 2:15, KJV)

MEDITATING UPON THE WORD OF GOD

Next, you must take your studying habits to a greater level. The word "meditate" means to engage in thought or contemplation, or reflect. Meditation is taking what you have already read and studied out and reflecting upon it. This will take you finding a place where you can just go and relax; a quiet and peaceful setting, where you can take that word that the Lord has given to you and seek His face in depth to what it is that He is trying to get to you. On this level, the logos, which is the written Word of God, begins to turn into rhema, which is the spoken Word of God. God will speak to you through His Holy Spirit and open up that word to you like never before. You will begin to receive greater revelation as you meditate upon the Word of God and you will begin to prosper in your life as God would have you to.

"This Book of the Law shall not depart from your mouth, but you shall meditate in it day and night, that you may observe to do according to all that is written in it. For then you will make your way prosperous, and then you will have good success."(Joshua 1:8)

MAINTAINING A LIFESTYLE OF WORSHIP

To love God is to worship Him. Worship can be done in so many ways because God is in everything that we do and He is everywhere in all things. Worship is not just singing to slow songs when we come to church. Yes, listening and singing to worship songs is a great way to set the atmosphere to enter into true worship, but there is much more to worship than just singing. God created us to worship Him. Worship is defined in many ways, but the one I will use for this text is to regard with ardent or adoring esteem or devotion. We can worship many things from our material possessions, to even a mere human being, but God is a jealous God. *(for you shall worship no other god, for the LORD, whose name is Jealous, is a jealous God, Exodus 34:14)* We are to worship nothing but the Lord and this can be done by reading the Word of God, taking time to spend alone with Him in prayer, taking care of the body that He created for you, loving others the way He loves them, giving to the poor, sacrificing your time for someone else, and many other things. In all that you do, see Him in it. In all that you do, make it a point to give Him entranceway into it. If He is the Lord of your life, you will acknowledge Him in every way, shape, and form that you possibly can think of. He must permeate your entire being to the point that He becomes a part of everything that you say and do. You must adore Him and honor Him with your life. Devote your entire life to Him. LIVE for Him!

"But the hour is coming, and now is, when the true worshipers will worship the Father in spirit and truth; for the Father is seeking such to worship Him." (John 4:23)

ABUNDANT GIVING

For God so loved the world that He gave...... As we purpose to allow the nature of God to abide in us, we must know that the utmost nature of God is to give. He gave His only Son to be put to death so that we could live eternally with Him. Is He asking us to give up our physical lives in response to this? No. What He asks us to do is to give our lives over to change and to live for Him in the earth. He desires that we allow Him to transform our sinful nature into the divine nature that we were created with. Not only this, God desires us to be givers in every area of our lives. This is how others will know that we are His; by how we give. We are to give of our time, our skills, our talents, our love, and yes, our finances. We are to offer all that God has given us to others. We are not to hoard anything that the Lord has blessed us with because we are blessed to be a blessing to others.

God will never release anything into your hands that is not attached to someone else. Your receiving a blessing from God is directly attached to someone else seeing His favor over your life and drawing unto Him. We are to seek the face of God for the gifts that He has placed on the inside of us, so that we can generate wealth for the Kingdom of God. God does not pour money out of the heaven supernaturally. He blesses us with a gift and allows that gift to produce wealth for the furthering of His Kingdom in the earth. As that gift prospers it will multiply, and as it multiplies, your giving should increase. Allow the gifts of God on the inside of you to cause an abundance of giving to pour out from you. As you give in abundance, God will continue to turn that gift every which way that it can turn on your behalf.

"Give, and it will be given to you: good measure, pressed down, shaken together, and running over will be put into your bosom. For with the same measure that you use, it will be measured back to you."(Luke 6:38)

SERVANTHOOD

The nature of God is revealed in many ways. He is our loving Creator and He has many facets to His nature. Jesus said in scripture that when you see Me, you see the Father. (John 14:7) We know that when Jesus began his earthly ministry at the age of thirty, He did not come across to many as someone who could be the Messiah; the Savior of the world. He possessed a quality that was taboo to many in that day because no one wanted to serve anyone but themselves. This still rings true to this day. We think that being a servant is to belittle ourselves and that servants are a less than honorable culture of people. Why did Jesus come into His ministry serving those who He would ultimately save? He was showing the character, or nature, of God Himself to the people. Servant is defined as one who expresses sub-mission, recognizance, or debt to another. There are other definitions that show of individuals being employed by another and this is fine, but this is not how God's nature of servanthood was revealed through Jesus Christ. He was revealing to others that to serve someone else was ultimately to love them. We must develop a lifestyle of servant-hood if we intend to bear the divine nature of God.

"For though I am free from all men, I have made myself a ser-vant to all, that I might win the more;" (1 Corinthians 9:19)

Begin today to incorporate all of these tools into your walk with the Lord. As you do, you will see His nature revealed in and through your life. Yes God wanted to save us so that we could live eternally with Him, but He has a greater purpose for you in the earth realm. Through a lifestyle of moving in His image, likeness, and nature, He will use you for the glory of the Kingdom of God. As these characteristics become a permanent fixture in your day to day life as an intercessor, the Lord will begin using you in ways that you could have never imagined. Will you answer the call?

ALL POWER AND AUTHORITY

"Then they were all amazed and spoke among themselves, say-
ing, "What a word this is! For with authority and power He com-
mands the unclean spirits, and they come out."

Luke 4:36

When you know who you are in Christ, nothing and no one can persuade you that you cannot operate in the full power and might of the One True God in the earth realm. When you understand the authority that God has released into your hands, you will begin to boldly move out and begin claiming the Kingdom of God over each and every individual that you come in contact with. The word power is defined as the ability to do or act or the capability of doing or accomplishing something. This word in the Greek is *dunamis*, which means force, miraculous power, ability, abundance, power, strength, and mighty work. The Lord wants to use you in the full power of the way He created you in the beginning.

As an intercessor, you are to go into the presence of the Lord with boldness and with confidence. If you are to effectively intercede and change the plans of satan in the earth realm, then you are going to have to possess the power needed to do so. We saw from earlier chapters that the power is in His Word and in His Spirit. All that you have to do is tap into that power and begin to boldly speak as the Spirit leads you.

SPEAK WITH BOLDNESS

As I stated earlier, when I began to intercede in a greater capacity, God began to send men and women of God into my life who either spoke a word of wisdom or even prophesied to me that God was telling me to be bold. I struggled with these revelations for weeks and even months, not knowing exactly what the Lord meant by being bold. Was I supposed to be harsh or rash? Was I supposed to speak as soon as I heard a word? Was I supposed to not take into consideration who I was speaking to according to their level of spiritual maturity? Was I supposed to quietly go before God and beg and plead for Him to intervene? All of these questions I asked of God. As I sought His wisdom and the wisdom of the spiritual leaders over my life, I began to receive my answers.

"Let us therefore come boldly to the throne of grace, that we may obtain mercy and find grace to help in time of need." Hebrews 4:16

Boldly in this text means out-spokenness, frankness, bluntness, publicity, and assurance. God desires for us to come to Him outright blunt when it comes to what we want to happen here in the earth realm. Now we understand that if we have been developed in all of the previously mentioned areas, then we will know the will of God and will only intercede according to His will. If this is the case, then God tells us to just "Do what you know to do!" We do not have to be timid or soft-spoken as we come before the throne of God. We reverence Him and honor Him, but I am here to tell you that you can dishonor the Lord by not taking a hold of the power that He has freely given to you in intercession. He needs men and women of God in the earth who possess the sheer power of His Spirit on the inside of them. He is counting on us to change the atmosphere of our families, communities, regions, nations, and yes, even our world.

Another definition of bold is frank utterance. We have to speak before something can happen in the earth realm. You can think about what you feel needs to change, but until you open your mouth, nothing is going to change. You have to have faith in God according to what you have heard Him say through His Holy Spirit and speak what He tells you to speak. I was so overwhelmed by some of the things that the Holy Spirit asked me to intercede for. I became inundated with fear because I did not feel as if I had the right to come to God in that manner. What I failed to realize was the relationship that God desired for me was that very type of boldness, knowing who I was; who He created me to be. I had to come to a point of understanding that I was no longer my own, but a servant to His will for my life.

"for which I am an ambassador in chains; that in it I may speak boldly, as I ought to speak." Ephesians 6:20

CONFESS WITH CONFIDENCE

Many people can be bold, depending on their specific temperament, but boldness coupled with confidence in the life of an intercessor is a powerful combination. Many people will say to you that you think that you are better than others, or that you are cocky, but when you begin operating in the full power and authority that God designed for you, people become convicted in their own lives. It has nothing to do with you personally; it just hits them where it hurts the most, because they are not living up to the potential that God created for them to walk in. God desires for you to show others the confidence that is in you through Jesus Christ. Confidence is defined as full trust; belief in the powers, trustworthiness, or reliability of a person or thing. This word in the Greek means reliance.

We know that there are many people in the world who are bold, but what is their boldness in? As believers, we are to possess boldness in the fact that we know who we are in Christ, but also confidence, or reliance upon the One who is doing the signs, wonders, and miracles. We come boldly before Him, fully relying upon Him to do what He said He would do.

"Now this is the confidence that we have in Him, that if we ask anything according to His will, He hears us." 1 John 5:14

When you know that you are only a vessel that God uses to manifest His will in the earth, you will lay aside all doubt, unbelief, and uncertainty and let God do what He has to do through you. Others may see this as pride, but when God receives the glory through your obedience, He will shut the mouths of your persecutors. When they begin to see that God is moving through you and that His anointing is upon your life, they will either hear you or they will run. They will either join you or they will come against you. Do not be distracted. It is not your job to please everyone and I can guarantee you that some will absolutely come up against you, but have confidence in the Lord your God and know that it is He who stands over His Word to perform it.

MOVE IN HOLINESS

As we discussed in Chapter five, Holiness in the life of an intercessor is absolutely necessary. We are to take every aspect of our lives and allow the Spirit of God to transform us into what He created in us in the beginning. We are being restored back to the original intent for us being created. We are learning how to move in the characteristics and nature of the One who created us and because of this, no devil in hell can stand up against us as we go before the throne of grace to intercede. What holiness does in the life of an intercessor is block the schemes and ploys of the enemy, rendering him ineffective as he tries to take our name through the mud. We have to guard ourselves and diligently keep ourselves covered. As you guard yourself and maintain a lifestyle of holiness, the enemy does not have any ammunition to throw your way.

"Having therefore these promises, dearly beloved, let us cleanse ourselves from all filthiness of the flesh and spirit, perfecting holiness in the fear of God." 2 Corinthians 7:1

A person who leads a lifestyle of holiness is someone to be reckoned with. As you submit yourself in obedience to the Father by leading a holy life, as He is, you give Him access into your life to move through you greatly. The power of God that was released through His Son Jesus as He moved in the earth during His three years of ministry is nothing compared to what He desires to do through you in this hour. The Word of God says, "Greater works shall you do because I go to my Father." (John 14:12) Jesus Himself said that you would do greater miracles than He did because He would be re-united with His Father; they were separated for a moment in time, but now they are fully conjoined in the power of God. He sits at the right hand of God making intercession for us daily. We have a power that is greater than the earth has ever seen before. Let us learn to move in this power by walking daily in holiness.

"And a great road will go through that once deserted land. It will be named the Highway of Holiness." Isaiah 35:8

LIVE IN VICTORY EVERYDAY

For the last three years, I have had the phrase Living In Victory Everyday spoken into my life. The ministry that God called my husband and me to is an awesome ministry. The set man of God of this house was given a mandate from God to transform and train believers to Live In Victory Everyday. He has poured into us consistently over the years to obtain victory in every area of our lives. I have taken these teachings and applied them to my everyday life and I have seen victory spring up every time that I have chosen to apply it. In the life of an intercessor, you are to know without a shadow of a doubt that the victory is already yours, because the Lord has already done it on your behalf.

"But thanks be to God, who gives us the victory through our Lord Jesus Christ." 1 Corinthians 15:57

This is probably the single gravest mistake we make as intercessors. The victory has already been achieved. When God calls you, He calls you from a completed state. What I mean is this; He does not ask you to intercede because the situation has not been resolved. He tells you to open up your mouth and agree with Him in heaven, so what is already achieved in heaven, can be made manifest in the earth realm. Glory to God! I can only speak out of experience. I used to become so overwhelmed because I felt the weight of the world on my shoulders because I thought if I messed up, lives would be lost and situations would worsen. What I failed to realize was that God had already obtained the victory in the situation when Jesus died on the cross. If I missed it, He would find someone else in the earth to agree with His word and cause it to manifest.

We should not take burdens upon ourselves that were not intended for us to carry. You should have full joy and peace in the Lord knowing that it is not you who obtains the victory, but God Himself. Where I believe we miss it is in not spending enough time in His presence to receive His heart on the matter. Just as I said in previous chapters, we move out too soon, instead of hearing what the Holy Spirit is saying. We would bypass a great deal of pressure, as well as anxiety, if we would just be patient and wait to hear what our assignment is. We have the capacity to Live In Victory Everyday if we would just trust in the Lord with all of our hearts and lean not to our own understanding. (Proverbs 3:5)

We must have faith in God and what it is that He is saying to us, cover what it is that He has said, and wait patiently on Him for the instructions. We cause ourselves to worry for nothing. Avail yourself to Him wholeheartedly, and He will allow you to obtain the victory in the earth realm, as it is in Heaven.

"For whatever is born of God overcomes the world. And this is the victory that has overcome the world—our faith." 1 John 5:4

The word authority is defined as the power or right to give orders or make decisions. Another definition says freedom from doubt; belief in yourself and your abilities. God created us in the beginning to have dominion. (Genesis 1:26) This word dominion is the Hebrew word *radah*, which means to tread down, subjugate, to crumble, have dominion, prevail against, reign, rule, or overtake. As intercessors, we should possess these very qualities if we are going to take back this world for the Kingdom of God. We were created to rule over all of creation and to cause the atmosphere to come in line with the word that is spoken from our very mouths. The same way that God spoke in the beginning and caused the elements to line up is the same power and authority that He has given to us to operate in the earth realm on His behalf.

God created us upright. He created all of the beasts of the field, the cattle, the birds of the air, as well as the fish of the sea from the same dust that He created us by, but why were we created to walk upright? The word upright is defined as erect or vertical, as in position or posture. This word in the Hebrew is *Yisrael*, which means he will rule as God. God's intention was to have someone in the earth that would look like Him, act like Him, speak like Him, and rule like Him; with all of the power and authority that He possessed in heaven. So He created man to walk upright, not only to distinguish him from the beasts of the earth, but to show that he was to rule over them, as God ruled in heaven.

"Truly, this only I have found: That God made man upright, But they have sought out many schemes." Ecclesiastes 7:29

Whatever it is that is not lining up with the word of God in your life or in the life of someone whom God has asked you to intercede for, has to be dealt with according to the knowledge that was given in the beginning. You have to know what He said about you and you have to know what He created you to be and to do in the earth. When you understand this through the knowledge of it in the Word, you then have to believe it, perceive it, and receive it! You have to become sold out to the fact that you have the power and authority to change the atmosphere around you. No matter where you go, you have the right to command things to change if they are not lining up with the will of God. God has given you the authority to bring heaven down to earth. You must accept this authority and begin to open your mouth and intercede for the nations. There is so much that is going on in our world today that was prophesied in the Word of God. We are standing in the final times of the history of this world and I get excited that God has allowed me to experience His power and authority in the ushering of His Kingdom in the earth realm.

"Assuredly, I say to you, whatever you bind on earth will be bound in heaven, and whatever you loose on earth will be loosed in heaven." Matthew 18:18

Whatever you ask God to remove in the earth realm, will be removed in heaven and whatever you send forth into the earth realm, will be sent forth into heaven. Do you see the power that you have in your mouth? An intercessor who is sold out to God, submitted under authority, and moving in pure holiness is someone who the enemy is deathly afraid of. This is why it is imperative that we possess boldness and confidence in this hour. You have no reason to fear the devil, because God has given you the victory through our Lord and Savior Jesus Christ. Just speak the Word over your life and over the lives of those whom God has entrusted to you and He will do the rest.

We just recently moved in our ministry from making confessions to decreeing them over our lives. The word decree means a formal and authoritative order, especially one having the force of law. Another definition is to ordain, establish, or decide by decree. There are some things that God desires for us as intercessors to decree in the earth realm. He no longer wants us to confess them, or say them over and over, but He wants us to decree them by deciding in our minds that it is done and that we believe it. Most often in the Body of Christ we see believers who are confessing certain things over their lives, but are seeing no real results. Why? Because they have not determined or made up in their minds that what they are saying is theirs. The atmosphere will only respond to authority. This is how the light entered into the heavens; by the power and authority of the voice of God. There are several instances in the Word of God where individuals spoke with authority and the elements had to respond.

We saw in the account of the prophet Elijah that he was a man just like us. He was not a superhuman, nor was he a spiritual being, but just a mere man who was tempted in the same ways that we ourselves are tempted. But he was submitted and committed and he understood the power and authority that God gave to Him to act on His behalf on the earth. It says in the word that he prayed earnestly. One definition of earnestly is demanding. Elijah placed a demand upon his prayers and God had to respond by sending the rain.

"The prayer of a person living right with God is something powerful to be reckoned with. Elijah, for instance, human just like us, prayed hard that it wouldn't rain, and it didn't—not a drop for three and a half years. Then he prayed that it would rain, and it did."
James 5:17-18a, MSG

This is so very powerful. We must know who we are in this world and we must understand what it is that God would have us to do for Him. My daughter came home one day and was so excited to share something that had happened to her and some of her friends as they were walking home from school. She shared with me that it was raining hard and that they wanted the sun to come out. She said that they all stopped and prayed hard that it would stop and guess what? It did! Do I believe that this is a coincidence? No, because I know and understand the power of prayer and the power of those who know who God is in their lives. I encouraged her that she has power in her words and that God has given us the authority in the earth to carry out His will. What did He do on that rainy day for those children? He increased their faith and caused them to seek Him more.

Another instance in the Word of God where someone used their rightful authority was that of the people of Israel. It says that they were given instructions by their set man of God, Joshua, and because they heeded his specific instructions, they came out victorious. The Lord spoke to Joshua and told him that He had already given him Jericho and that all he had to do was give the instructions and carry them out accordingly, and that the wall of the city would fall.

"So the people shouted when the priests blew the trumpets. And it happened when the people heard the sound of the trumpet, and the people shouted with a great shout, that the wall fell down flat. Then the people went up into the city, every man straight before him, and they took the city." Joshua 6:20

From the authority of the voice of their man of God and the power in their voices, they took the city of Jericho, just as God had promised. We must know that there are outside influences that support us as we heed the voice of God through intercession. The Word of God tells us that we all have been appointed angels that stand guard over us, but there are also angels of war who move out only on the powerful and authoritative voice of a believer. All throughout scripture we can see the intervention of angels in the lives of the people. In the instance of Jericho, Joshua did his part by giving the people what God said. The people did their part by heeding the instructions and carrying them out to the point of shouting with power and authority. When that power was coupled with the authority of God's voice, there were angels of war released to tear down the walls of Jericho. We have to understand that when we stand in agreement with the Father in the natural, then there are entities standing in agreement in the spiritual.

As people of faith, we understand that the worlds were framed by the word of God and that the things that we see were not made by things visible to the eye. (Hebrews 11:3) We must exercise that faith daily in our walk with the Lord, so that we can increase that faith to carry out His perfect will in the earth. All God asks us to do is agree with His word by faith and then do something with that faith. Faith is an action word. We must not only say that we have faith, but we must activate that faith by carrying out a corresponding action, so that the angels assigned to that specific situation can move out and carry out God's will for that situation. We are not alone people of God. God said that He would never leave us or forsake us. (Hebrews 13:5) Just as God needed to send Jesus into the earth realm to occupy a body for the redemption of mankind; He needs a body in the earth realm to carry out His plans in the earth. This is why He created Adam and Eve; to have dominion and to have His voice present in the earth. Without the voice of God present in the earth, there is darkness. It was not until He spoke that the light entered the world. Glory to God! The only way for things to change in the world today is if you open up your mouth and begin to declare what the Lord is telling you to say.

When you begin to operate in the full power and authority that God created you with, there is not a demon in hell that can hinder you from carrying out the will of God. The devil, as well as his demons, know the voice of God and just as the angels respond to power and authority by moving out on that word, satan and his demons will retreat and run from someone who in walking in this authority. It is only when you are not convinced of the power and authority that dwells inside of you that you become overwhelmed and worry about the outcome of intercession, instead of boldly declaring in obedience and letting God handle the rest. Just as we saw earlier, there are only three areas where the enemy tempts us; one being that of the pride of life. The devil would have you to believe that God is speaking only to you and that you have to take this heavy burden upon yourself to "make things happen" in the earth realm. It is not about you! And you are not the One performing the signs, wonders, and miracles. It is God Himself. You are just agreeing with His Word and causing it to be released in the earth. If you do not know His word and are timid with the word that you do know, the enemy will laugh you to scorn. This is how he torments us as intercessors. He causes you to put the focus on yourself when you should have had your focus on Jesus.

There have been several times in my walk with God where I took my eyes off of Jesus, not intentionally, but I allowed the situation to overwhelm me, because I thought that the full burden of the weight was supposed to be upon me. I caused myself undo stress, anxiety, and confusion because I did not understand how to hear from God and wait patiently for His instructions before moving out. Again, it was me, not God. If we understood our "position" in the scheme of things, we would not step into a position that was not ours to begin with. If Eve would have understood her "position" in the Garden, then she would have known that God had already given her all the desires of her heart. Why? Because He created her. It was only when the deceiver entered in and questioned her about what she really wanted that she was tempted. We have to know when to speak and when not to speak. The devil does not know your weaknesses until you make it available. You do not have to say it out loud, "Hey satan, I am weak in the area of my finances!" No, you can just be sitting alone in your house and declare "out loud", or into the atmosphere, that you are broke. Because you released that word in the open, satan's radar honed in on your "house", and now he will begin to tempt you in this area.

We must possess the wisdom of God. You must know your enemy and how he maneuvers for you to be effective in the ministry of intercession. Many may tell you that all you need to know is the word of God and you will be fine, but that is not what the Word of God says. In 1 Peter 5:8 it says:

"Be sober, be vigilant; because your adversary the devil walks about like a roaring lion, seeking whom he may devour."

This is his job; to seek out those who are not on their assignment; those who are not standing their watch for the Lord. Bishop Steven W. Banks says it this way in his book *Apostolic Gatekeepers*[7]:

There is no rest for the watchman ministry. Someone is always on guard making continuous intercessions.

If you are on your post and vigilantly watching for the enemy, you will not be devoured. The word "vigilant" means keenly watchful to detect danger; wary or ever awake and alert; sleeplessly watchful. This is the exact tactic that satan uses in the life of an intercessor. The Lord will wake you up in the early morning hours to intercede because there are specific watches of the night, and each of these watches has a varying degree of authority based upon the tactics that satan uses during each watch. You must be aware of what your watch is and know the degree of intensity that the Lord would have you to intercede. When you become aware of this, then you will be better equipped to handle whatever it is that the enemy may throw your way. This fight is not a physical one, but a spiritual one, but if you do not guard yourself and allow the Spirit of God to move through you, you will feel as if you have gone through a physical fight. Now there are times during intercession that you will stand in the gap and go on the offensive on behalf of someone or for a situation. I have been in times of intercession where when I came out, my stomach muscles hurt, my voice had become scratchy, and I just wanted to find somewhere and go to sleep. As I stated in an earlier chapter, these are times of travailing in intercession where you are literally birthing something into the spiritual realm, just as a baby is ushered into the world through travail.

Please know that the enemy is not just going to stand by patiently and let you do this. He will send out his demons to try and thwart your plans, but you must press forward even greater and wail on behalf of the situation. You must be as that mother bear that carefully guards her cubs from danger. If anything tries to come near and steal that cub away, she goes on the offensive and attacks. I have travailed in prayer to the point of exhaustion, but in the end I knew that God had prevailed over the situation. You will know when something breaks in the atmosphere over a place when intercessions are going up before the Lord. Please be prepared to be one of very few who will operate in this authority. Some are skeptics, including many inside of the Body of Christ, but this is just a distraction from the enemy to curb you from fulfilling your call from the Lord. If there is only one submitted and obedient vessel in a congregation, God will use you mightily for His glory. God was not able to find this submitted vessel, so He brought salvation through His own body.

"He saw that there was no man, And wondered that there was no intercessor; Therefore His own arm brought salvation for Him; And His own righteousness, it sustained Him." Isaiah 59:16

This is not so in this hour. We have been redeemed by the Father and He has given unto us His Holy Spirit. He is calling us to intercede in the earth, but again, not too many people have received the revelation of intercession. He will begin to show Himself through you to the people, so as to draw them into the power and authority that they too possess on the inside of them. You must be faithful to what it is that God is telling you to do and not worry about what others are not doing. As you remain obedient, God will draw them.

The assignment of the intercessor is to go on the offensive and take territory for the Lord. The enemy's job is to kill, steal, and to destroy, (John 10:10) so we must take back from him all that he has stolen from us or from those whom God has us interceding for. You must be mission focused and understand that you have an assignment to carry out for God and that nothing and surely no one, including satan, can stop you. God has given us dominion and no matter what our circumstances may look like, that will not change. The Word of

God says, "Forever O Lord your word is settled in heaven." (Psalm 119:89) So if His word is settled, then I have to settle it in my mind and do what He tells me to do. We see so many times in scripture where God commands someone to do something for Him, but before He does, He always tells them that He has already done it.

*"**See, I have** set the land before you; go in and possess the land which the LORD swore to your fathers—to Abraham, Isaac, and Jacob—to give to them and their descendants after them."*
Deuteronomy 1:8

*"Now the LORD said to Joshua: "Do not be afraid, nor be dismayed; take all the people of war with you, and arise, go up to Ai. **See, I have** given into your hand the king of Ai, his people, his city, and his land." Joshua 8:1*

*"**See, I have** divided to you by lot these nations that remain, to be an inheritance for your tribes, from the Jordan, with all the nations that I have cut off, as far as the Great Sea westward." Joshua 23:4*

*"**See, I have** this day set you over the nations and over the kingdoms, To root out and to pull down, To destroy and to throw down, To build and to plant." Jeremiah 1:10*

This is so powerful and if we could understand that when He calls us to intercede for a person or a situation, He has already gone before us and made the pathway straight for us to go in and retrieve the territory, and to receive the victory. God gives us the power and authority to enter into intercession with boldness and confidence, not in ourselves, but in Him. Jeremiah 1:10 said, *"I have set you over the nations and over the kingdoms."* The word nations in this text refer to the heathen and the word kingdoms in this text means dominions. We understand that the kingdom of darkness has its own dominions and we must be in position to do just what Jeremiah says, "to root out, pull down, throw down, build, and to plant. We are not a people without power or without authority. God has freely given them to us, so that His will can be manifested in the earth realm.

As an intercessor, you must have knowledge in the area of the spiritual realm. There are many different spirits that operate in the realm of darkness and you should be able to discern over time when a spirit is in operation. This allows you to intercede on a greater level of authority. When someone is ignorant to the spiritual realm, or when they have not been trained or taught in the ways of the spirit realm, the enemy will laugh at them because they do not hold weight, or authority. We saw in scripture many times where Jesus commanded the demons and devils to depart out of certain individuals. He did not sit there and have long discussions with these people, but with His authority, commanded them to leave, and they left. When you enter into intercession, you may come up against certain spirits that will try you because you are 'trespassing' on their territory, if you will. Please know that the enemy is not just going to sit idly by and watch you destroy his kingdom. He too has power, but it cannot compare to the full power and authority that you have in God. Study your adversary and guard yourself as you stand in the gap for the Lord.

The ministry of the intercessor is one of the most important ministries on earth at this time. There is so very much taking place in the world and God needs men and women of God strategically placed around the globe to intercept satan's ploys. We need to know who we are and who gave us the authority to operate in the earth realm. Now we know that Jesus was human, as we are. For Him to be able to operate in the earth realm on behalf of His Father, the Holy Spirit had to be released into his earthly body. Glory to God! Even though He was God, in the earth realm, He had to adhere to the physical limitations in His earthly body. The release of the Holy Spirit into His earthly body allowed Him the power to operate on earth, as it was in heaven. He was able, through the power of the Holy Spirit, to lay hands on the sick, cast out demons, and to heal all forms of disease.

We know that even as a young child, He possessed great wisdom and He sat among the elders and scholars of the land, but it was not until He reached the age of thirty that He received the gift of the Holy Spirit. It was after this point, where the scriptures tell us that He began to preach with power. (Luke 4:32) The same is true for us. We are spiritual beings in an earthy body, but this is not a limitation. With the help of the Holy Spirit, Our Helper, we are able to take down the kingdom of darkness in the lives of our families, our friends, our communities, our nation, and all over the world.

There are many different strongholds that have taken root in people's lives. Whether it is a *"generational curse"*, *"sins of the father"*, or a *"territorial demon"* that has taken advantage of a nation's tragedy and plundered them into depression or suicidal thoughts; you have to be ready to combat that stronghold by identifying the "strongman", or root of demonic influence. Once you are able to pinpoint that first area of reference, you can enter in to root out, pull down, throw down, and then begin to plant and build back up with new foundations of godly influence. As an intercessor, God has equipped you to carry out His plans in the earth realm. As you stay before the presence of the Lord in prayer, meditation, worship, and so forth, you give Him a place to "set up shop". He is looking for willing and obedient vessels who will just allow Him to do His job through them.

There are so many demons being released into the earth realm at a greater level than we have seen before. The Word of God says, "In the last days, I will pour my Spirit upon all men..." (Joel 2:28) The enemy is very aware of the word of God and knows that his time is short. He too is sending out whatever means he has to devour the world before they can see the Light of the word, but we have to begin taking territory for the Kingdom of God. As I said earlier, this has to be done on the offensive. We cannot afford to just sit back and wait for the enemy to move before we take a stand. We have to always be on guard making continuous intercessions for the saints and for the world.

One of the ways that the Bible references intercession is through the hands. Hand in the Hebrew is the word *yawd*, which in one of its definitions means dominion. Throughout scripture, we see instances where men and women of God were told to clap their hands to either thwart off the enemy or to enter into battle. Clapping of the hands in intercession is an avenue to confuse the enemy. Hands, being significant of dominion, cause the enemy to retreat. He understands the power of the hand of God and that the same power was transferred to man in the Garden. This specific power was taken from the serpent when the curse was imposed upon it in the Garden. The Word says God cursed the serpent by causing it to go on its belly. This implies that the serpent, at one time, had either "hands" or feet that gave it the power to maneuver greater in the Garden. Because God created man in His image and likeness, he possessed not only the upright position of dominion, but the "hands" of intercession in the earth.

Why do Christians wait *until* something happens to go into warfare or to intercede for situations around the world? This should be a LIFESTYLE for the believer. God strategically sets watchman over neighborhoods, cities, countries, and nations to root out and to pull down; to destroy and to throw down; to build and to plant. You have been sent by God to the city where you are. The Word exhorts us to pray for the peace of the city where He has sent us. (Jeremiah 29:7) Are we taking our posts? Are we standing on the walls of our cities? Are we held up in the watchtowers with our lights shining brightly?

No matter how challenging the task may be that God has as-signed you to, it will never be greater than the power that He has provided for you to carry it out. He will never call you to intercede for a situation where He has not already supplied the necessary tools for victory! Let us take our eyes off of ourselves and keep our eyes fixed on Him and know that He has overcome every situation that we can ever think of. He has already mapped out the ending; we just have to walk it out in the natural. You must know that God is with you every step of the way and He is just a prayer away if you need Him. He is your Father and He has your back. Stand boldly and declare His perfect will over the earth. You play a major role in the establishment of the Kingdom of God. Do not take your position lightly. Know that you are called by God to do something that not too many people are willing to do.

I believe that God is calling a new generation of intercessors to the forefront; those whose hearts are sold-out to Him and sold-out to changing this world for His glory. They are tired of "church as usual" and are ready to establish the Kingdom of God in the earth. He has a great assignment with your name on it and has given you the power and authority to carry it out. Will you answer the call?

"CALLING ALL PASTORS":
COVER THE INTERCESSORS

"Let all things be done decently and in order."

1 Corinthians 14:40

When I first began the journey of this book, this chapter was not even an afterthought in my mind. In fact, I thought that this would be the title of my next book. As I was in London meeting with a publisher, he confirmed that this was the heart of God, and that He needed this chapter to be included in this book. As I prayed and talked with the Father, He released the word for this chapter. As in most areas of the church, intercession is a not so talked about gift amongst the crowds. For far too long, the church has been placed under worldly restrictions that were never intended by the Father. From church deacon boards who vote in or vote out pastors, to trustees who are telling the pastor what he or she should be doing with the money in the church; the Body of Christ has lost the order that was ordained by God for the house of the Lord.

Many may reject this word, but it is necessary for the fulfillment of the Kingdom of God to become established in the earth. The house of the Lord is supposed to be the "light", or the example to the world, but it has become tainted and dulled over generations, because of pride, greed, and in many instances, just plain ignorance. We have been comfortable with religion and traditionalism, and have not allowed the Spirit of God to have His full office space within the house of the Lord. We have allowed mere man to choose what goes on in God's church without allowing His divine input to rule and reign over every other opinion. Because of this, the church was split into denominations that were never intended to be so by God. Again, I know that this will not be an easy pill to swallow by many, but God will receive the glory!

From the Pharisees to the Sadducees, we can trace back through our pasts to the exact roots of skepticism to the Gospel that was preached by Jesus. These were the *"deacon boards"* of that day; the Sanhedrin. These were men who followed strict religious laws from the Mosaic Law, but who, in reality, even though they claimed to abide by these strict laws; themselves forsook most of these laws. Jesus called them "hypocrites". They challenged mostly everything that Jesus preached in his earthly ministry from who Jesus ate with, to why His disciples did not fast as they did, to saying that Jesus was casting out demons by Beelzebub, and not believing in angels or the resurrection. A total of one hundred and five times in the Gospels are the Pharisees and Sadducees mentioned. Why did the writers of the Gospels find it so very important to mention them so many times? Because when the Truth is preached, and when believers are walking in the full power and authority that Jesus taught us to walk in, the naysayers and the "hypocrites" will begin to come up against it.

We are moving into a time in our history where those very teachings, which Jesus gave to us before He ascended to sit at the right hand of His Father, are being manifested in the lives of His Sons. No matter what denomination you are a part of, and no matter what laws are a part of your church, God is causing order to become established in the house of the Lord once again. The gifts of the Spirit are beginning to re-emerge in the church, and God is going to have His way. Yes this is going to cause a rift amongst many traditionalists and the religious, but the Word of God says that *"He is coming back for a church with no spot or wrinkle"*. (Ephesians 5:27)

Church as usual is coming to an end. Planned programs, services, and the like, will become a thing of the past and give way to the Spirit of the Living God to operate how it is that He sees fit. Now God is a God of order, and it is He that sets those in the body as it pleases Him. The most important aspect of this is that of the "set" man/woman of God. All throughout scripture, we see that when God desired to move in the lives of His people, He would call out a man/woman and give them the vision for the people. The set man/woman would then give the people exact instructions from the Lord on how to carry out the vision. We saw several times in the Word of God what happened to certain individuals who did not obey those instructions, and who tried to move out on their own, without the leading of the man/woman of God, including Miriam and Aaron to name a few. It is absolutely pertinent that we follow proper order in the house of the Lord, and God is not in the business of having *"loose cannons"* in His church.

"For God is not the author of confusion but of peace, as in all the churches of the saints." 1 Corinthians 14:33

Intercessors avail themselves greatly to the Holy Spirit, and because of this they are hearing many things from Him. As we reviewed in the earlier chapters, they must know when to speak and when not to speak, but this is not left in the hands of the intercessor himself. If God desires to release a Word to the church through an intercessor, He will speak to the set man/woman of God through His Spirit and then they are released. As we saw in the beginning; everything must be done decently and in order.

The ministry of intercession is a progressive ministry. Most people who move powerfully in the area of intercession possess the prophetic anointing upon their lives. As a pastor of someone who is operating in the ministry of intercession, as well as the prophetic; God is calling you to cover that anointing. Now this has not been an easy task for many men and women of God in the past, because they have somehow allowed this to 'threaten' their authority as the pastor? As I stated earlier, God sets those in the body as it pleases Him.

As a pastor or leader of a congregation of believers, you have been graced with the gift to lead that people, and the office of the pastor and such does carry the authority to govern the gifts of the house as it pertains to order, but you must be willing and obedient to allow the Spirit of the Living God to move freely, without hindrance, in the lives of His people. This takes a great deal of spiritual maturity and the discernment to know what God has called you to do and what He has not called you to do. If your vision is all about God, then you will allow His Word to govern every aspect of your ministry. The Word of God in Ephesians Chapter four makes it very plain:

"And He Himself gave some to be apostles, some prophets, some evangelists, and some pastors and teachers, for the equipping of the saints for the work of ministry, for the edifying of the body of Christ," Ephesians 4:11-12

So we see that there are differing gifts in the house of God, but that they are for the equipping of the saints, and for the edifying of the body. Your entire goal as the set man/woman of God should be that of spiritual growth and maturity in the house, and for God's purposes to be made manifest there. You have to be willing to put aside all of your own opinions and your own insecurities and allow God to be God through whomever it is that He chooses. You should mainly be concerned with that of fulfilling the call that He has placed upon your life. Our man of God has told us so many times before; God gives us grace to perform the gift that He has placed upon each of us. If we are trying to move in a gift that He has not graced us with, then we will not only become frustrated, but we can cause great damage to the body of Christ.

You have to know who you are and what your own assignment is for the Lord, in order to stand in agreement with what God is doing in this hour through His intercessors. God is raising up a new generation of believers who are completely sold-out to Him and His will in this earth. They are seeing prophetic fulfillment all around them, and it is not going to take them five, ten, or fifteen years to catch a hold of God's plan, as it did for many of us. They are going to begin moving greatly in the prophetic realm and in the power of His Spirit in sheer holiness. These are those who will be on fire for the Lord and nothing and no one can persuade them otherwise. You have to be willing to lay aside all religion and tradition and jump on the boat as it steers toward the ushering of the Kingdom of God into the earth.

Now this can only take place if your ministry is in tuned with the Holy Spirit. Many traditional churches do not move in the gifts of the Holy Spirit, nor do they allow the Spirit of God to flow through them. They preach the Word of God, but choose to omit certain instances in the Word of God as it pertains to the Gift of the Holy Spirit, as well as the evidence of speaking in tongues. If we are going to see the manifestation of the signs, wonders, and miracles spoken of in the Word of God, then we are going to have to allow the Spirit of God back into our churches. We are wondering why our churches are not growing. We are wondering why people's lives are still in shambles within the body of Christ. We are wondering why there are no real instances of healing sick bodies, opening deaf ears, opening the eyes of the blind, and raising of the dead. Why? Because the Spirit of God cannot operate in 'dead bodies'. Glory to God! By this I mean spiritually dead bodies; without the Holy Spirit.

For too long we have allowed men and women to come into our churches and corrupt them. Instead of being a leader to the people that God has entrusted to us, we have allowed them to come in and begin setting up their own visions, instead of the one true vision that God gave you as the head of that ministry. It does not matter if you only have three members in your church; if God has not released them to operate in a certain capacity, you cannot elevate them into a position that they are not spiritually ready for. We have churches who have memberships with less than one hundred members, and over half of them are in leadership positions and are preaching from the pulpit their own visions, instead of the vision of the set man of God. There are 'self-professed prophets' who are coming in and prophesying to your members, without you knowing "whose" they are. This is becoming *"the thing to do"*; calling in "Prophets" to speak a *"word from the Lord"* to you and your members, but even this in many cases is not God.

Let the Spirit of God enter into your ministry, and let Him speak to you, as the man/woman of God over that house, what it is that He wants to take place in that ministry. Stop allowing rogue members to dictate to you what should be taking place in the house that God entrusted to you. If everything falls apart, guess who is held responsible for it? This also holds true in the instance of not allowing the gifts to operate as they are supposed to in the church. If God has spoken to you that an individual in the ministry is called to any specific office or that they are to be operating in any specific anointing and you refuse to elevate that person, you are in direct rebellion to the Spirit of God and you will be held responsible. The Word of God says it so wonderful in 1 Thessalonians:

"And we urge you, brethren, to recognize those who labor among you, and are over you in the Lord and admonish you,"
1 Thessalonians 5:12

As pastors, you must know those individuals who are among your congregation who are faithful, willing, and obedient. Many times, God will not just right away reveal to you those whom He is calling out for the ministry. More often than not, it will be just you seeing the faithfulness of a member, and therefore elevating them into leadership capacity. From here, you will see God moving through them, and God will give you a discernment of what it is that He has called them to do for Him. I am here to tell you that there are many unsuspecting pastors, prophets, and evangelists who stand in our children's ministries Sunday after Sunday who are content with just serving God's precious little children. They stand in our parking lots, creating order before the people even enter into the doors of the church. They greet and usher people at the door with a spirit of discernment to know where and "where not" to sit them. These are individuals who would rather be standing at the door of the house, than to be outside in the world. Pastors, you must be able to see these individuals for who they are, and guide them and lead them into the perfect will of God for their lives.

When I first knew that God was calling me into the ministry of intercession, I received a word from my woman of God that He was calling me out. Now I prayed all of the time and I really did not know the extent of what she was saying. I thought that prayer and intercession was the same thing. Many of these precious souls have no idea of what God is calling them to do. They are ignorant, if you will, to the process of maturing in this gift. There needs to be spiritually mature leadership within the house of God who can nurture the gifts on the inside of these individuals. The Word of God will absolutely teach and serve to mature the believer, but there are times when only experience is the best teacher. Now for those of you who have already established intercessory prayer groups and meetings, you must be sure that those who are leading these meetings are Spirit-filled and called by God to be operating in this ministry. These leaders should be able to discern when God is moving in the life of an intercessor. They should be able to guide them and lead them during the process, and give them their own experiences, while allowing the Spirit of God to move freely in that individual's life.

There is no real protocol in the life of an intercessor, because the Spirit of God moves differently in every gift, but order is the one true ingredient that can never be left out. The intercessor needs to know how to operate in order, and they need to know their boundaries within the church setting. When these establishments are set in place, it allows freedom within the house of the Lord, and allows great moves of God to take place in the church. I can only speak from my own experiences. Our pastor is a man that is truly led by the Spirit of God. When I first came to this church, I immediately witnessed the freedom of gifting in our church. He was ministering the Word of God, and then he just stopped. There was a woman who stood up, began speaking in the "gift" of tongues, and then she interpreted her own tongue. The power of God shot through that entire sanctuary, and he said that was it. He stopped preaching, and said that nothing else needed to be said. This display of the Spirit showed me the liberty that operated in the midst of this congregation. He understood that it was not about him and what he desired, but what God wanted and what God desired. He was confident in what God called him to do, but he was also cognizant of the call on this woman's life, and what God desired to do through her to speak to His people. He was not hell-bent on having service after God had already spoken. He recognized that

God wanted to come down and sup with His people through this gift, and He did just that. This is spiritual maturity!

This is the kind of spiritual maturity that God operates through. When we all understand that God has set us in the positions that He graced each of us for, then we will not be frustrated, unhappy, or covetousness of another's gifting. Now many of us will not believe that there are pastors who are jealous of the anointing on their members' lives, but it is a sad reality. This takes place even in the confines of the pastoral marriage. One partner may be more in the forefront than the other and this, if not dealt with, can cause division. Again, you must know what it is that God is calling you to do. What we fail to realize is this; if you begin trying to operate in the anointing of another, the grace that God gave to them is not upon you. You will eventually begin to show signs of phoniness, because you have stepped out of the will of God for your own life.

Why am I saying all of this? Because there are some men and women of God who have coveted the gifts of their own members. You have to check yourself daily, and test yourself to see if you are in the faith.

"Examine yourselves as to whether you are in the faith. Test yourselves. Do you not know yourselves, that Jesus Christ is in you?— unless indeed you are disqualified." 2 Corinthians 13:5

Just because you are a pastor or head of congregation does not mean that you hold the full authority for what goes on in that house. You must be submitted fully to your head, which is Jesus Christ, and to the leading of His Spirit to show you how to build His church. You are just a covering for that house. You are a vessel that must be submitted to the will of God for His people and in that, you must be willing to step out of the norm if that is what God is calling you to do. You cannot be conformed to what everyone else is doing, because God is building an army who has to combat the enemy on many different fronts. Not every ministry will have the same anointing, but they must all operate in the order of God for that particular anointing. There should be intercessors in every house of the Lord. There should be someone who is standing in the gap on behalf of the set man/woman of God, as well as the assignment for that house. These individuals are the most targeted by the enemy. Why? Because they threaten and confuse his plans. As a pastor, you should welcome the intervention of the intercessor. We are so very in the dark as to the assignment of those whom God uses in this capacity. We are not fully aware of the sacrifice that comes along with this anointing.

We saw in scripture many instances in the prophetic books how God used the 'intercessors' of that day. Every prophet from Isaiah to Malachi had a passion on the inside of them for the people of Israel. They hated evil and wanted to see God's purposes manifested in the lives of His people. Regardless of the people's rebellion, each prophet continued in their assignment to bring the Word of the Lord, but this did not come without great sacrifice on behalf of each one of them. These are men who cried out to the Lord literally for the people, some of whom were imprisoned for their obedience to God, and even one who lay on his side for a total of three hundred and ninety days. Now I am not saying that God is asking intercessors in this day and time to go to such extremes, but who am I to say what He would and would not do; He is God! The point that I am trying to make is this; cover the men and women who are standing in the gap in your ministry. Feed them, train them, and lead them into the very call that He has predestined for their lives, so that His perfect will becomes evident in your ministry, your community, and all over the world.

If you have not started an intercessory prayer group in your church, I admonish you to seek the face of God in this area, and allow His Spirit to lead you. Intercessors stand as watchmen over ministries, communities, regions, territories, and nations. Just as there are territorial demons standing over an area; there are intercessors that God has called to root out, pull down, tear down, and literally obliterate the plans and purposes of satan in that area. Your job is to guard them and seek the face of God as to how He desires to use them in your ministry. As I began operating in the ministry of intercession, there was no covering over my life. I mostly interceded in my home; in the confines of my four walls. I was not aware of the extent that God was using me, until He began to show me the results of those times of intercession. I am now under a great covering, and I do know that my man and woman of God pray for me and cover me. I know that they cover the call and anointing upon my life, and I also know that they will not release me to do anything that the Holy Spirit has not led them to release me to, and I am so grateful for that!

Many people desire to move out into their calling by any means necessary. As pastors over their lives, you should encourage them to go through the process and allow God to mold them and transform them into the vessels that He is able to use for His glory. I believe that we all need to be taught, but more importantly, I believe that we need to be trained. There should always be someone with experience and someone with a greater anointing upon their lives to train the next generation to walk in their gifting. We saw in scripture where Abraham passed the torch to Isaac, Isaac to Jacob, Moses to Joshua, Elijah to Elisha, and so forth. The Word of God says that the anointing flows from the head down. We need to be training the next generation of intercessors to stand under the anointing that is upon our lives, so as to fill their cups until they overflow with the Spirit of God, and with the prophetic anointing needed to recover lost territory for the Lord.

The ministry of intercession is a very powerful ministry. As an intercessor avails himself/herself to the Lord, they are literally bringing God's heart into a situation or into an area that previously contained darkness. They enter into the realm of the spirit and shake the kingdom of darkness and take by force what the enemy has stolen from God's people. They are standing in the gap for peoples, places, and situations; agreeing with heaven's purposes; sometimes laboring for hours and even days in continuous intercessions. Now there are different assignments for each intercessor. If you have an intercessory prayer leader set in place, this person needs to be spiritually in tune with the heart of God and be a great discerner. They must be able to recognize when someone has been sent to intercede for a specific area and not hinder this individual in that particular assignment. They all work together in harmony, but just in different capacities. For example, you may have someone who is there to specifically cover the entire intercessory prayer meeting. This individual/individuals may only lift up the leader and the other intercessors in the group, so as to keep the conformity of the service flowing. They may pray for unity and oneness within the entire group, so that God's plans will succeed during the meeting.

You may have another intercessor that will only cover the leader of the group. God may have called them specifically out to lift this leader up before the Lord that they have eyes to see and ears to hear what the Spirit is saying for the meeting. They may cover his/her family as well. This too, can be an assignment of more than one intercessor. Next, you have the intercessor that has been placed within that group to do warfare on behalf of the meeting. There are people that will come into a prayer meeting with no intentions to pray or intercede for what is on the heart of God, but they are sent to cause division, confusion, derision, and to just outright hinder the purpose of the intercessory prayer meeting. These intercessors can 'spot' or recognize when someone has come into the meeting and subsequently, if they are gifted in the area of the prophetic senses, are able to discern the spirit in operation and right there bind that spirit before it can interrupt the flow of God.

The intercessors who are called to this type of intercessory assignment are great discerners. The meeting can be in progress and these intercessors can walk in and just sense that it is not in order. They will immediately go into warfare, binding up whatever spirit has come in or been let into the meeting, intentionally or just by an intercessor who has not lifted their own issues up to God before praying. Now, do not be intimidated by this type of intercessor, because they can become very 'passionate' in their warfare. By this, I mean that they can get louder in their intercession and they may clap their hands loudly in an effort to confuse the plans of the enemy, as we discussed in the earlier chapters. Now there are many who get out of hand with this and put on a great show for you, but this is not of God. Some call them "flaky" intercessors, and I have been in the midst and seen this myself. But when someone is genuinely moving in the area of spiritual warfare and prophetic intercession, the entire group will sense it and also enter into great intercession.

As I said earlier, everything should be done decently and in order. The Spirit of God brings order with everything that is birthed from the heart of God. Now, I need to make a much needed statement here. This is only in the case of a spiritually mature intercessory group. There have been times when I was a part of an intercessory prayer meeting where the Spirit of God was just there by Himself. By this, I mean that the power was not activated in that meeting due to a lack of knowledge, wisdom, or discernment of the intercessory prayer function. Yes, they were praying and yes, God heard their prayers, but the power of God to change situations and circumstances was not present. The boldness and confidence that characterizes the intercessor was not there. So, if you are an intercessory prayer group leader and you have not taught these individuals what intercession is or in some way been an example to the power of God yourself in these meetings, then you are hindering greatly what God is able to do through you and this meeting. You may have a new member come in and have the fire of God on the inside of them to 'tear up' the plans of satan in such a meeting, and because you are not used to this, you may think that they are crazy or even as they called Jesus, Beelzebub himself. You must gain the wisdom of God in the area of intercession and you must submit yourself wholly to the Spirit of God, in order for results of intercession to be made manifest.

This is where a pastor comes in and this is where hearing from the Spirit of God is paramount for your church/ministry. You have to know that those who lead these intercessory prayer groups are capable and qualified to do so. Now, there is not a class in place that could teach an intercessor to do *all* that God has placed inside of them to bring His plans and purposes to pass. But we would be wise to incorporate such classes to better equip new believers and those who may have come from other ministries who have never been in this type of setting. There are so many facets to this ministry that we are ignorant in regards to. There are times when the prophetic giftings may show up and someone will release the Gift of Tongues and subsequently, interpret as well.

As I said earlier, I have been in such a setting and it is a powerful display of God's Spirit. You have to be willing and spiritually mature to know who among you has such a gift and if so, you need to give them the room to be used by God. Prophesy can also come forth in such meetings and this can be the Word of God specifically for that meeting, but if you are not open to let God use whom He chooses, then you are hindering the entire meeting.

As pastors, you need to set leaders in place who are spiritually grounded, faithful, and known as intercessors themselves. You should be covering these individuals with your prayers and support. You are to be the fathers and mothers in the faith who undergird their call, as they stand in the gap for you and the ministry. The office of the shepherd is one of servanthood; to lead, guide, and nurture those in whom God has entrusted to you. It is not only important to teach us, but what is more important is to lead us as a father would.

"For even if you had ten thousand others to teach you about Christ, you have only one spiritual father." 1 Corinthians 4:15a

Now I want to encourage each pastor reading this to seek God's face concerning obtaining a group of intercessors to cover you and your ministry. If you have not already, begin asking God who He has sent to cover you; they are there. We have seen too many pastors and leaders in the church falling into temptation over the past decade, as we have never seen in history before. Satan's tactics are becoming more and more obvious in the lives of our pastors. With church growth soaring, there are many flocking to the house of God, but don't get so excited just yet; they are not all sent by God.

There are those whom the enemy uses to enter into the church to cause confusion, derision, division, and just out-right nastiness. We are seeing more and more people who are coming to church with different motives. You have to be prepared and be on guard to discern who is for you and who is not. You have to seek God's wisdom in this area, but as a pastor, because you have so many obligations already on your plate, this may be an area that you will have to turn over to the intercessors in your church.

I read a book by C. Peter Wagner entitled *Prayer Shield*[8], and in this book, Wagner has revealed a substantive study done on pastors all over the world over many years span and the outcome reveals that the majority of pastors that fell into temptations were the direct result of not having personal intercessors praying for them. We see men/women come in the church who prey on the pastor. They already have it set in their mind that they will do everything in their power to test and tempt the man of God. This "spirit" is that of a Jezebel spirit; it seeks to diminish the anointing on the man of God's life through tearing his name down among the people of God. The Jezebel spirit operates in the midst of the leadership of the church and does not concern itself with mere lay-members, even though a form of this spirit can operate in anyone's life. The entire purpose of this spirit is to bring down godly authority over communities, regions, and even nations.

I came across this spirit for the first time about a year ago. I had been taught concerning this spirit in one of our previous ministries, which gave me insight and knowledge into how it operated, so I knew it immediately when confronted with it. The woman had a drawing character to herself; not one of contagiousness, but one of control. I saw her cause men to flock to her, and after a while, I realized that these were all Christian men. I could not for the life of me understand how naïve these men could be, but then God began to really open my eyes to the schemes of satan.

This woman had a previous connection to our ministry, but left for a while and then returned. She would not attend the ministry, because she stated that the anointing that was on the set man/woman of God previously was great and that the new leadership was beneath her. My spiritual "antennae" went up immediately. From this moment on, I watched and prayed concerning this woman. I began to see more men that I knew become entangled by this spirit. She also began to visit the church from time to time, and every time that she did, my spirit was thrust into intercession. The Lord spoke to me that this woman was there to test and to tempt the man of God, and to bring shame to the church through the men in this church.

Pastors, there are times when you will not see these spirits, because you have been placed on a different mission; to preach the Gospel. You have labored many hours and days; sitting before the face of God to get the Word for His people. You are sent out in great capacities to other cities, states, countries, and nations to minister the Gospel and many times, as C. Peter Wagner states in his book, your prayer life is not what people think it is. Let's be transparent here. If we are going to be delivered and set free from bondage, we are going to have to address the not-so-easy topics that we are embarrassed to admit.

"Therefore let him who thinks he stands take heed lest he fall."
1 Corinthians 10:12

There are pastors who, instead of humbling themselves and recruiting faithful intercessors, put on a façade to make their members think that they have it all together, and that they are exempt from being tempted by satan. Don't be naïve or foolish; this is not about you. There are wives, husbands, children, and your members who can and will fall into the hands of satan if you fall. We have seen it happen. People have left churches that they have attended their entire lives, and never return, because their man/woman of God has, in their eyes, betrayed them through their choices. They put you up on this pedestal where they believe that if anyone can resist satan, it is you. They look to you to be that foundation of security for them. They know that if you can do it, then they have a chance to as well. Now, we understand that every walk is a personal one and every Christian is responsible for their relationship with God, but there are spiritually immature Christians sitting right in your church every Sunday who do not get this. No, it is not your job to be Jesus for them, but it is your job to do all you can do to make sure that you guard yourself, your family, and that ministry. You are held responsible for its success, as well as for its demise.

It is possible. You can be covered to such an extent that your life, your marriage, and your ministry does not have to become a statistic to the world. But it is going to come from a place of spiritual maturity, as well as humility to acknowledge that you cannot do this on your own, and to accept that God has ordained specific intercessors to cover your life, your marriage, your children, your finances, and yes, your ministry.

Do not be afraid of change, and do not be intimidated by the fire that is on the inside of these intercessors; these sons and daughters in the faith. Do not run them away, but welcome them with open arms and cover them, but make sure that they are trained to move in proper order, as it pertains to the Spirit of God. You serve a greater role in their lives than you know, and they too serve a role in your life as well. God has entrusted them into your hands, and given you all that you need to teach, train, and lead them into His perfect will for their lives, as well as a larger role in the church, the community, and yes, the entire world. Will you answer the call?

NOTES

Introduction

[1] Dr. Joe Ibojie: Dreams and Visions Copyright © 2005 Destiny Image Europe, Pescara, Italy.

Chapter 1

[2] Page 23: Dr. Will Moreland. International Gospel Church Kitzingen, Germany "Show the House to the House" 2008 www.igcgermany.org

Chapter 4

[3] Page 63: Charles Haddon Spurgeon. A Passion For Holiness. http://mikeratliff.wordpress.com/2007/03/17/charles-spurgeon-quote-on-holiness/

[4] Page 71: Dr. Kristie Moreland. International Gospel Church Kitzingen, Germany "Separate Yourself: Be Holy" 2008 www.igcgermany.org

[5] Page 78: What Will People Say by Hilary June Amara Copyright © 2007 Xulon Press Longwood, Florida.

Chapter 6

[6] Page 100: Dr. Will Moreland. International Gospel Church Kitzingen, Germany "The Image, Likeness, and Nature of God" 2008 www.igcgermany.org

Chapter 7

[7] Page 128: Bishop Steven W. Banks: Apostolic Gatekeepers Copyright © 2008 Expanding Your Vision Publishers Virginia Beach, Virginia.

Chapter 8

[8] Page 147: C. Peter Wagner: Prayer Shield Revised Edition Copyright © 1992 Regal Books Ventura, California.

Contact us:

Hunter Heart Publishing
P.O. Box 354
DuPont, Washington 98327

publisher@hunterheartpublishing.com

(253) 906-2160

www.hunterheartpublishing.com